GHOST
Hunters'
Guide to
Sheffield

Valerie Salim

Sheaf Publishing • Sheffield

GHOST HUNTER'S GUIDE TO SHEFFIELD is published in a new, revised edition in 2001 by Sheaf Publishing Ltd, 191 Upper Allen Street, Sheffield 3

ISBN 1 85048 020 6

Where to start your Ghost hunt

Introduction

SINCE I WROTE the first guide to Sheffield's ghosts, there have been many changes in Sheffield.

Some of the places noted in those earlier books no longer exist. Ghost-hunters will look in vain for the the the Hole-in-the-Road and the old Britannia Music Hall. The site of Middlewood Hospital is being redeveloped. Abbeydale Grange and Holt House has been demolished. Are our ghosts an endangered species?

Fortunately, we can point to the refurbished Lyceum Theatre, the Royal Victoria Hotel and many other places where ghosts are still making their presences felt.

I am not a professional ghost-hunter, but a collector of local stories about strange, often unexplained, phenomena. I began my research with an open mind on the reality of ghosts, but since hearing so many perfectly sober, respectable and normally unimaginative citizens describe their weird experiences, I am in no doubt that there is some other world, or worlds, whose inhabitants are able to interact to a limited extent with ours.

I leave the question 'What are ghosts?' to professional psychic researchers and to the host of brilliant philosophers who have debated the subject down the ages. Are they proof of life after death or creations of the Devil, souls not yet passed over or only wicked likenesses of dead people, conjured up to deceive us? The reader must decide for himself.

I have kept as far as possible within the official boundaries of Sheffield, but if the locale of a particularly good story is just a mile or two outside, I have sometimes included it. This collection, however, is not to be read by those of a nervous disposition, alone before a flickering fire at midnight, for the ghosts of Sheffield, far from being the products of the uneducated, superstitious imagination of a bygone age, flourish in this materialistic, industrial, fourth-largest city in England. They are not restricted to Gothic piles in the depths of the countryside, but are to be found even in modern council houses. They need not be anonymous white ladies or monks, but perhaps Uncle George come back to enjoy a pint with his old mates.

At most within ten minutes walk of your own safe, comfortable home, dear Sheffielder, a poltergeist may be at work or a grey form forever haunting the scene of a tragedy.

Once again I must thank the staff of Sheffield Central Library for their invaluable help in illuminating obscure corners of local history, and also everyone who put me on the track of ghostly neighbours.

Sometimes I came across stories in old books or newspapers, or people told me what someone else had told them. Inevitably from mouth to mouth, as in the children's game, some facts are missed out and others distorted or rationalised according to the listener's own experience.

Where possible I tried to sort out what really happened. Because a fact had become distorted in the telling, it did not mean there was no basis for it.

After I first wrote about Sheffield's ghosts in the 1980s, several readers said that they would appreciate a more detailed treatment of the historical background and I have here tried to satisfy them. All my original entries have been checked and brought up to date.

Some of these stories are guaranteed to chill the blood, some to start a tear or two and some may even raise a smile. Our local ghosts are never boring, as readers will learn.

Valerie Salim
September 2001

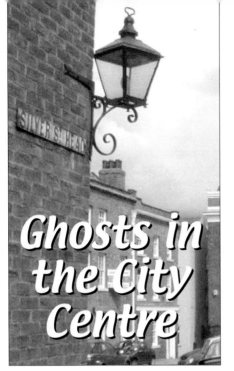

Ghosts in the City Centre

Sheffield Cathedral and High Street

....

A TUNNEL, now blocked at both ends, runs from Boots' basement across the junction of High Street and Church Street to the Cathedral.

Probably part of the tunnel was lost when the pedestrian underpass, filled in again in 1993, was constructed in 1969. There was a delay in completing the stairs at the cathedral side when workmen found coffins dating from the 1500s. The Provost of the Cathedral was not surprised, stating that most of Church Street was a graveyard years ago. 'You cannot dig anywhere between the Cathedral and the Town Hall' without finding coffins.'

Were the more recent apparitions disturbed by the removal of their coffins, or are they the same as those reported at the end of the last century under Hartshead?

When workmen laying the track for the Supertram in Church Street in 1994 dug up more coffins, did they start up more ghosts?

At the Cathedral end, the verger could only guess that a small door in the eastern wall once led into the tunnel. Ghosts, however, are not deterred by underpasses and blocked up doorways. It may be that the same spirit wanders between the two buildings and in the Cathedral amuses itself by blowing out candles and re-lighting them, and switching lights on and off when there is no human being there once the building has been locked up for the night.

Many people have sensed a presence in various parts of the building, including the Shrewsbury Chapel at the eastern end. A cleaning lady at work in the Sacristy suddenly became aware that she was not alone and glimpsed something white out of the corner of her eye, but when she turned around, no-one was there.

We do not know when the first church was built in Sheffield, although the early ninth century Shefffield stone cross – now in the British Museum – is evidence of Christianity here back then. There is no mention of a church in the 1085 Domesday Book, but it may have been destroyed during William the Conqueror's devastation of the north in 1070, when the manors of Sheffield and Hallam suffered badly.

About 1100, William de Lovetot, the Norman Lord of the Manor of Hallam, built the church, some of whose stones are now in the walls of the Chancel and Sanctuary, and which was damaged or maybe destroyed in 1265.

The present Perpendicular style church was built in the early fifteenth century, with seven altars.

The central tower still stands today, but the cruciform plan was altered in the reign of Henry VIII, when in about 1520 the Lord of the Manor, George fourth Earl of Shrewsbury built the Shrewsbury Chapel with a vault underneath.

On the opposite side of the High Sanctuary a wooden shed stood outside for many years, housing the town fire-engine, until in 1777 at the petition of the Vicar and Church Burgesses to the then Lord of the Manor, the Duke of Norfolk, a fine new extension was built in its place, St. Catherine's Chapel, with a vestry below and a room above for the Church Burgesses.

However, from the time of Elizabeth the gloomy Nave was allowed to decay until, a complete shambles, it was pulled down and rebuilt. The new Nave, completed in 1805, was an architectural disaster, but was improved in 1880 by being extended to 175 feet in length. A new West door was added with porches to the north and south, and also the north and south transepts. The old galleries were removed and new pews installed. The Chancel floor was raised and re-paved and the organ removed from above the three-tiered pulpit into the space previously occupied by the Vestry and Church Burgesses' Room.

In 1913 a new diocese was formed and Sheffield Parish Church was given the dignity of becoming a Cathedral. After the First World War, plans by Sir Charles Nicholson were approved to transform the old church to suit its new title, but nothing was done until 1935, when he was asked to prepare new plans to enlarge it.

The nineteenth-century Nave was to be demolished and a large new one built at right angles to it with the main entrance in Church Street. The foundations were actually laid and work was to begin on 4th September 1939, but war was declared the day before and the contract was cancelled. After the War, indecision and delay saw ever-mounting estimates, until in 1961 the Nicholson plan was finally abandoned.

However, in the three years before the War the new Chapter House, Song School, Vestries and St. George's Chapel were completed and other work on the north side continued, with such labour and materials as were available, until autumn 1942.

After 1961 the existing west end was pulled down and re-built to lengthen the Nave by another 28 feet. The porch and main entrance were now entered through an open Narthex with a tower, to harmonise the new building with the old. The Sanctuary of the Chapel of St. George was converted into the organ chamber and the new chapel placed between the Chapel of the Holy Spirit and the north wall of the Nave instead of a new High Altar and Sanctuary. The Cathedral was rehallowed on 15th November 1966 in the presence of the Archbishop of York.

Perhaps the Shrewsbury Chapel (since 1935, officially known as the Sanctuary of the Lady Chapel) is the main attraction for the Cathedral's ghost, if she is indeed Mary, Queen of Scots, whose gaoler, the Sixth Earl of Shrewsbury is buried there. Some say the ghost is the Earl himself.

The tunnels which are uncovered by workmen throughout the city from time to time are usually described by local historians rather unromantically as old drains or old mine workings. Whatever their original function, the city centre is riddled with them. Undoubtedly, the local inhabitants put the secret passageways to good use, not only to avoid foot-pads.

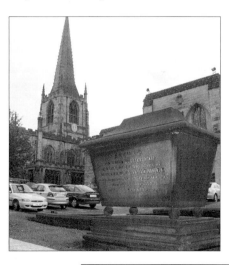

Hartshead

....

IN THE DAYS when the racing newspaper, *Tissue* was printed in the basement of the Tramway Club, Hartshead, near the present offices of *The Star*, a printer's labourer hard at work heard the clanking of a chain. He thought the sound was made by his mate. Then, a minute later a man in ancient dress, wearing a hood, came from an unused cellar, carrying a bucket as if it contained water. The man walked past him and seemed to go clean through a stone wall. The labourer's yells brought his boss running, who thought he had been drinking and threatened to sack him.

Frank H. Brindley, the historian, heard the story and in 1855 excavated at the spot where the ghost had passed through the seemingly solid wall. He found a tunnel cut from the rock, six feet high and five to six feet wide, going eastwards towards the Castle. The floor was well worn and dry. He followed the tunnel to a point under the Argos store, where it was forty-feet below street level and under the sewers. There they found that it had been bricked up, probably in 1830, when foundations were being dug for new buildings. On the rock was cut the inscription, '*I.W. 1830, B.R. and T.W.W.B*'.

The ghostly old-time workman who walked the tunnel was usually seen alone, but was sometimes leading a lady (whom some naturally identify as Mary, Queen of Scots). He carried a vessel, which he dipped into the crystal-clear waters of the well that Brindley discovered, after lifting a flagstone, four feet below the cellar floor of a building on the site of the old Tramway Club. The well was sealed in 1916.

The entrance to the tunnel from the cellar was found guarded by a heavy oak door with iron bolts when workmen broke into it in 1896 while digging deep below the old *Shades Vaults* tavern. (In the 1830s known as the *Shades* – an ominous name!) It was entered down a flight of steps from Watson's Walk, where Argos is now.

Of the inscription *I.W. 1830, B.R.* and *T.W.W.B.* cut on the rock, *B.R.* may refer to B. Richards and Sons, tailors, who occupied 59-61 Market Place from 1830 into the 1880s, and whose basement extended from the front of Market Place to the middle of Hartshead and the entrance of the *Shades Vaults*. The tavern and Cockaynes were both bombed during the 1940 Blitz.

It was probably part of the same network of tunnels that a *Sheffield Daily Telegraph* reporter investigated in 1896, when High Street was widened. A workman digging new drains showed him a three-foot wide ancient tunnel between five and six feet high which ran in a direct line between the Castle and the Parish Church. It led into a crypt-like cellar, which had once been used by a wine-merchant, probably as far back as the Middle Ages.

The workman brought the reporter up more modern cellar steps into a derelict building. This tunnel seems to have run about where the Vulcan Travel Agency in the Hole in the Road was once situated. Naturally the small, narrow office had a ghost, but she was not Mary, Queen of Scots. When the subway was built in 1967 the place was a storeroom for a sweet kiosk, but was a travel agency between 1973 and 1986.

Valerie Maples, the manageress of Vulcan Travel, described how at the beginning of 1983 for two consecutive days there was a mysterious dialling sound coming from the telephone, even when no-one was near it. Then, a week later, for four days the staff were assailed by a stench they variously described as being sweet and buttery or like dried blood. They cleaned out all the desks and disinfected and sprayed to no effect, but suddenly the stench disappeared of its own accord.

At the northern end of the office there used to be a bench for the use of customers. Ten weeks after the incident of the stench, two assistants on different occasions (the second not having been told anything by the first) saw an old lady sitting there. She was dressed in a brown bonnet with a frilly blouse. Soon afterwards, the bench was ripped out and a window put in that section. Six months later the old lady appeared again on the same spot, this time standing. She was not seen again.

The Hartshead tunnel, with its two ghosts, ran in a south-westerly direction with quick turns all the way. It came out in the cellar of the building on the corner of Fargate and Norfolk Row, now occupied by Next.

The site was once occupied by the Lord's House (Lord of the Manor). After Sheffield Castle was demolished in 1646, the Lord's agent and occasionally the Dukes and their families resided at the Manor House. When that was dismantled in 1706, the modest-sized house in Fargate was built instead, with gardens going right back to Norfolk Street.

In the eighteenth century Henry Howard, agent to the Duke lived there, and his son, Bernard Edward was born there in 1765, to succeed his cousin as the 12th Duke of Norfolk. One room was used for Roman Catholic worship, and when the house was pulled down in 1815 a small chapel was built in the grounds with its entrance on Norfolk Row. Up to 1850 it was the only Catholic place of worship in Sheffield. St. Maries' church was not built until 1846-50.

With such a history and despite the tunnel entrance now being blocked, it comes as no surprise to learn that in the spring of 1985 a shop assistant in the cellar of Next was scared half to death by what she described as strange noises among the coat-hangers. The staff only later learned of the tunnel and its ghosts. There have been no odd happenings there since 1990 at least.

Lyceum Theatre

Tudor Street

A MAP OF 1736 shows only fields on the site. Later there was a drill ground, and after that gardens in front of the house of Henry Tudor. Even later there was a bowling green (Arundel Street was once known as Bowling Green Lane), and by 1865 it was a drill ground.

By 1884 the site had been cleared and a large wooden circus erected, *The Grand Theatre of Varieties*, with E. S. Drake as proprietor. At some time between 1879 and 1890 the father of Dan Leno, the famous comedian, ran a Pavilion of Varieties here next to the theatre.

In 1890 Sheffield Corporation had taken over the *Grand Varieties Circus*, with Alexander Stacey as lessee, it being also known as *Stacey's Theatre*.

In July 1893, the site having been cleared, the foundation stone of the present splendid theatre was laid, and it was opened on 26th December of the same year, seating 2,000 people and with a

proscenium 32 feet wide. It was then known as the *City Theatre* and Alexander Stacey was listed as the proprietor.

In 1897, however, it was taken over by The Sheffield Lyceum Theatre Ltd, and re-opened under its new name.

The exterior was designed by Walter Emden of London and Messrs. Holmes and Watson of Sheffield, with the interior designed by W. G. Sprague, the famous theatre architect, who was also responsible for the *Wyndham's*, *Globe* and *Aldwych* theatres in London's West End. The interior plasterwork was applied directly onto the walls when it was wet, in a process pioneered by a Sheffield company. Michael Denison, the actor, called it 'a Stradivarius among theatres'. Henry Irving, Ellen Terry and Anna Pavlova were among the famous stars who appeared there.

Unfortunately, by the 1960s audiences dwindled as people stayed at home to watch television. Like so many cinemas and theatres around the country, the proud *Lyceum* was turned into a bingo hall, although pantomime survived there until 1969, when Vince Hill starred in 'Dick Whittington'. But in 1972, despite a 17,000 name 'Save the Lyceum' petition, the theatre closed.

As a result of a public enquiry in 1975 the Department of the Environment made a Preservation Order to save the interior, but it remained empty despite various proposals to re-open it as an entertainment centre. In 1981 it did re-open as a rock venue but closed again in January 1982. The Lyceum Theatre Trust, backed by the City Council, was formed to bid for the theatre, but their bid was unsuccessful and it seemed that the *Lyceum* would become a night club. However, that venture failed and the building was again for sale. This time the Trust's bid was accepted.

One of the best things to come out of Sheffield's decision to bid for the 1991 World Student Games was the necessity to spruce up the city. A theatre of such architectural importance as the *Lyceum* standing derelict was not a good advertisement for Sheffield's cultural heritage.

Fortunately the intricate rococo plasterwork on the stalls, boxes and proscenium arch remained intact and only needed to be re-gilded and re-painted once the roof had been weather-proofed. The foyer was re-designed and also the backstage area, providing new dressing rooms, offices and rehearsal rooms and housing the Sheffield Theatres Education Department. Restored to its Victorian glory at a cost of over £12 million, with grants from Sheffield City Council, the EEC, English Heritage, sponsors and public donations, the *Lyceum*, with its deep stage and clear views for every member of the audience unobstructed by supporting pillars, a feature of all Sprague-designed theatres, is a top regional venue.

Before the theatre closed down there were many reports of strange happenings. Staff often resigned after unnerving encounters, warm rooms suddenly turned cold and a stage-door man claimed to talk to the apparitions, including Ben, an old-time stage-hand.

In December 1981 some electrical work was necessary before it could open as a rock venue. The later landlord of the *Ship Inn* told how he and his mate were working there, the landlord in the gods and his mate in the balcony. At lunchtime they met on the balcony to eat their sandwiches and his mate complained that a man had been watching him all morning. Irritated he had told him to b– off, but the man had taken no notice. He had a handlebar moustache and carried a cane. He wore a straw boater, striped jacket and light-coloured flannels. Another workman, who had been listening, exclaimed 'Do you know who you're describing? That was the Lyceum ghost!' It was a former manager, who has also appeared near the dressing-rooms.

During the restoration work, which began in March 1989, the ghosts were scared away, but since the re-opening in

December 1990 they have now happily settled back into their renovated home.

The ghostly star turn is a young woman in an old-fashioned grey dress, who occasionally appears in the No.1 star dressing room and at the rear of the balcony. She is said to have hanged herself from the balcony after a visiting actor from the D'Oyley Carte Company promised to marry her, but then abandoned her when he moved on to the next town.

In February 1992, Matthew, who worked in the office, was walking in the corridor near the dressing rooms, when he felt someone put a hand on his shoulder. He looked round. No-one else was there!

The Star offices

York Street

WHEN *THE STAR* staff moved into their new offices across the street at the end of 1994, it soon became clear that there were already other presences in residence. On two occasions mirrors leapt into the air and one shattered on the floor behind a receptionist. Staff also detected an unpleasant stench like rotting vegetables.

Psychic Gary Wilson thought there was nothing to worry about. He sensed a little old man with half-moon glasses, which fitted the description of the tailor, who was there thirty years previously when it was the shop of Wilfred Lyons, established 1895, Saville Row tailor. Mr Wilson also sensed a little girl aged between eight and ten with long blonde hair. There is an eerie feeling in the cellar and staff don't like going down there for stock.

Psychic Bryan Hillerby thought that the spirits may have been disturbed by recent renovations and the removal of gravestones from the Cathedral yard during work on the Supertram tracks.

'Someone or something is trying to get out,' he said.

Boots the Chemists

4 High Street

THERE HAS BEEN a chemist at No.4 High Street since at least the middle of the nineteenth century. The Sheffield Directory of 1856 records a J. Wick, druggist and a Samuel Coulson, agent there, while H. Hawkin, milliner, had No.6.

In 1868, Cubley and Preston, chemists and druggists, and G. A. Roberts, dental surgeon had taken over No.4. In 1888, Walter Nield, photographic apparatus manufacturer, was sharing No.4 with the chemists, but by 1896 he was the sole occupant.

The foundations and basement were incorporated into the new building constructed about 1898 by the well-known local firm of architects founded by William Flockton, which was responsible for many city buildings, including the Town Hall, Ecclesall Union Workhouse (later Nether Edge Hospital), the Cathedral extension and Norton Chapel.

Boots Ltd, chemists and stationers, now occupied No.6, while No.4 was occupied by the Thatched House Restaurant. In 1905 Miss Mary Smith, victualler, was at No.4. The *Thatched House Hotel* survived from 1913, when Mrs Emily Bentley was manageress, until 1930. Then Boots acquired the whole site and replaced the old building with its present one in 1933.

The Territorial General Manager has apparently not heard of any poltergeists connected with Boots, but the staff working there are aware of unusual happenings in the basement stockroom.

In 1980, Mr Allison was working as a porter at Boots. One of his tasks was to collect 'cages' full of goods from the stockroom to take to the sales floors and to return the empty cages. The stockroom, the oldest part of the shop, was said to be blocked off at one end, concealing a tunnel which led under the street to the nearby cathedral. The stockroom was approached through an outside door, with a small, cluttered alleyway leading off, and a narrow passage with glass stacked on shelves on either side.

At least one shopgirl refused to go into the stockroom unless the lights were all switched on, and the place certainly had an eerie atmosphere, especially in the early morning when Mr Allison started work. He preferred to wait for a cleaner to arrive before he went in there.

The head porter told him that, on opening the shop, he often sensed a presence, as though he were disturbing something. On one occasion, while walking through the stockroom, he heard something thud onto the floor behind him. He turned and saw that a bag of flour was lying burst open in the middle of the floor, several feet away from the shelf where it had been stacked. At other times, doors leading to the stockroom would slam violently shut, even though there was no draught.

A part-time security attendant on night-duty had an Alsatian with him. As they approached the stockroom the dog began to howl and the hair on its back bristled. The man was so frightened that he locked himself and the dog in an upstairs office until daylight.

Mr Allison himself was one afternoon returning to the ground floor from the stockroom. It was raining heavily and the atmosphere was gloomy with the threat of thunder. Walking down the passage to the outside door, he was thinking only of the miserable weather, when a piece of glass, which had been neatly and safely stacked, flew sideways and was hurled by some unseen force violently to the floor a foot in front of him. His first reaction was amazement, then he laughed, then, suddenly afraid, he yelled and ran upstairs to the ground floor, where he told everyone what had happened.

Happily, the hectic throngs of customers in the busy shop during the day keep the unseen resident in the basement. He (or she) likes peace and quiet.

Wicker Herbal Stores
117 Norfolk Street

ABOUT THE MIDDLE of the eighteenth century the Trustees of the Norfolk Estates began the development for building purposes of the agricultural land then known as Alsop Fields.

No.117 Norfolk Street, at the corner with Surrey Street, dates from about 1765, its first recorded occupants being Messrs. Faulkner and Magnall, variously described as merchants or factors, in 1781.

Hibbert Bros. fine art dealers, were founded by William Hibbert in 1834 in Fargate and moved to 117 Norfolk Street in 1842. They owned the premises until the Second World War, when the council took it over. Hibbert's rented it ever since, but on March 28th 1998 Hibbert's closed

down. The shop remained empty until February 2000, when it re-opened as the Wicker Herbal Stores, with a vegetarian café upstairs

In the cellar there were for many years mortuary slabs from the nearby old Medical School. Could spirits accompanying them be the reason why, in the left-hand corner of the shop facing the door, after a sudden noise items on display would drop down?

Cutlers' Hall

Church Street
....

C UTLERY HAS BEEN produced in Hallamshire since at least the thirteenth century. In 1297 Robert the Cutler of Sheffield was listed in a tax return. Sheffield's reputation was considerable by 1340, when a Sheffield knife was listed as one of Edward III's prized possessions and in the 1390's, when Geoffrey Chaucer wrote his *Canterbury Tales* – the Miller of Trumpington in the Reeve's Tale bore a 'Sheffield thwitel in his hose'.

At first the Manor Court controlled the cutlery industry, supervising the system of apprenticeship and trying to maintain standards, but by 1590 a separate Cutler's Jury was established. They eventually decided to apply to Parliament for an Act of Incorporation, which was given the Royal Assent on 23rd April 1624. This Act established the constitution of the Company of Cutlers.

At first the Cutlers met in a rented room, according to tradition the upper room of a stone-built town house in Fargate, later the *Cutlers' Inn*. In 1638 however they decided that they needed their own building. It was built of stone with a slate roof on the same site as the present one in what was then Church Lane, for £155-15s-10d.

This Hall was demolished in May 1725 and a second Hall built for £430-10s.

In 1776, the Cutlers decided to rent a piece of land on which to build a new Hall rather than repair the old one. The Duke of Norfolk's agent wanted a ground rent of £22 a year for land near the present Town Hall. The Cutlers would pay no more than £21-13s-3d, so the Hall remained on its present site.

However, by 1827 this second Hall was in a disgraceful state 'unworthy of the Company to whom it belongs'. So in 1832 it was demolished and the present Hall was built. It was jointly designed by Samuel Worth and Benjamin Broomhead Taylor. The building cost £8,846-12s-1d and the furnishings £1,092-3s-2d. In 1867 it was extended by the addition of the Banqueting and Hadfield Halls and in 1881 the facade was extended westward. It is now a Grade 2 Listed bulding and is considered to be one of the finest Livery Halls in England.

It is used not only for the annual Cutlers' Feast and general Cutlers' business, but also for many other functions including weddings and exhibitions.

The worthy cutlers are a dignified company and nothing must be allowed to diminish that dignity, so employees must not talk of any strange happenings at the Hall. They admit only to feeling a Presence, even when they know that they are alone in a room. They quickly look over their shoulder, but can see no-one.

St. James' Church

St. James' Street

··

THIS CHURCH, so badly damaged during the Blitz that it had to be pulled down, stood at the top of St. James' Street, near the Cathedral, where there is now a car-park.

It was erected by subscription for £3,000 in 1788 as a chapel-of-ease to the parish church on part of the glebe land belonging to the vicarage. The square, stone building was in Grecian style, with two rows of square windows with a cornice ornamented by vases. At the western end was a tower with a cupola supported by pillars. Inside there was seating for 700 people, including the galleries which rested on cast-iron pillars. Over the communion table at the eastern end was a window portraying Christ on the Cross.

None of the pews were free. Each share of £50 entitled the subscriber to a pew as a freehold inheritance. The rest was auctioned off. It was one of the few churches built in modern times to have vaults for the burial of the dead, although some were buried in the churchyard too. Subscribers were given preference for burial in the vaults, where the charge was five guineas – just over five pounds – in 1824.

During the War, the vaults were broken into and three of the forty-six tombs were opened, perhaps by thieves hoping to find jewellery on the corpses. Were they interrupted by the ghost said to guard the vaults?

When it was decided not to rebuild the church, which in any case had become redundant, the corpses were re-buried elsewhere and the vaults filled in.

Leader House

Surrey Street

··································

AT THE END of Surrey Street, its fine Georgian façade overlooking Arundel Gate, stands Leader House.

A little before 1760, Thomas Leader, a fine silversmith, left his Essex home to live in Sheffield, where with Henry Tudor he founded in 1762 the firm of Tudor, Leader and Company, silver platers, specialising in snuff boxes.

In 1777, he leased from the Duke of Norfolk the house which from that time was known as Leader House.

After 1788 the house was altered by the addition of a bow window at the north side and the back premises were changed considerably. The house passed to a number of owners, one of whom, Marmaduke Wardlow, did much restoration work.

In 1939, it was bought by Sheffield Corporation, who in 1970 wanted to demolish it to use the site for the new Register Office. Fortunately, permission was refused, as it is a listed building.

Leader House's permanent resident is reputed to be a servant girl although

no-one in recent years has met her face to face and her exact story is not known. The staff are, however, agreed upon one thing – that the old house has a very creepy atmosphere, and unaccountable happenings have made many of them nervous of going upstairs.

Mrs Edith Mosley, a cleaning lady, described how, when she was interviewed for the job, the interviewer said, 'I hope you are not of a nervous disposition'. In fact Mrs Mosley was the only one who would clean the top floor, despite the fact that she herself in 1978, while working in the end room, which was probably a servant's bedroom in the old days, felt 'cold sweep round my face'. There were no windows open to cause a draught. She was not afraid, but felt it unusual enough to tell the rest of the staff about it.

Another cleaning lady was walking up the stairs to the top floor when she heard footsteps following her, but there was no-one there. The porter's dog refused to go into the end room – surely a sign of some unusual presence to which animals are supposed to be especially sensitive. The cellars are said to have the most spooky atmosphere. Gas and electricity meter readers certainly prefer a member of staff to accompany them down there!

Leader House became the Sheffield Development Office, accommodating Destination Sheffield and the Sheffield Visitor and Conference Bureau, but staff saw nothing unusual. But perhaps they didn't get up early enough.

An employee at the Novotel, Arundel Gate going on duty in the early hours of the morning saw what may have been the Leader House ghost, a faceless grey figure in the road outside the Surrey and Fringe moving in the direction of Leader House.

Leader House has since been refurbished and opened on April 5th as the administrative headquarters of The Millenium Gallery.

Novotel
Arundel Gate
······················

WORK STARTED ON the hotel in 1990 and it opened in February 1992 with 144 *en suite* rooms, and conference and banqueting suites catering for up to 200 people.

In 1994, a German man was found dead of a heart attack in his room on level 5 and on another occasion a man was found dead in his room on level 2.

Staff find the fifth floor much quieter than the other floors. It has quite a spooky atmosphere and they feel that they are always being watched. Sometimes they have heard their names shouted, but no-one was there.

The chef was on the fourth floor, when he heard someone on the floor above running up and down, but when he went up, no-one was there.

A chambermaid said she avoids looking in mirrors, afraid of what she might see looking over her shoulder, particularly in the bathroom en suite where the German died. The television sometimes turns itself on when no-one else is in the room.

Town Hall
······················

IN THE MIDDLE AGES Sheffield town was governed by the Court of the Lord of the Manor, presided over by the Lord's Steward. In 1297, however, Thomas Lord Furnival gave Hallamshire its Charter and the Free Tenants some say in their own affairs. By the 16th century they had their own Court of Sembly Quest, which met on Assembly Green (now the Wicker). The

Burgery of Free Tenants was responsible for maintaining roads, bridges, the archery butts, the pillory, gibbet and ducking stool as well as the maypole, and overseeing the watchmen and constables. In 1682 they became the thirteen town trustees.

According to Harrison's survey of Sheffield of 1637 the Town Hall had 12 tenanted shops underneath, rented for 2s to 28s a year. The small building erected in 1700 with the Duke of Norfolk sharing the cost, in the south east corner of the Parish Churchyard was of brick, with the gaol on the ground floor, while the town business was conducted upstairs. It had a small belfry with a gilded ball on top.

The population of Sheffield increased rapidly during the Industrial Revolution as people from rural areas came after jobs, but the town government did not keep pace.

In 1808 a new Town Hall was built at the corner of Waingate and Castle Street, putting the town into debt, and unable to afford tackling problems such as drainage and inadequate housing. However in 1818 two Acts of Parliament dealt with the provision of gas street lighting and gave the Trustees the power to levy rates and set up a small police force.

Conditions in the slums only improved slowly and the police force was badly undermanned. The penny-pinching trustees decided they could not afford to build public toilets, a museum, or a lunatic asylum.

At last, however, conditions did improve. Sheffield's population was almost 334,000, when in 1893 it became a city. The slums of the Crofts between the Parish Church and West Bar were demolished as were rows of houses at the corner of Pinstone Street and Surrey Street, for the city had to have a new Town Hall. The old building was given over entirely to the law courts.

The new Town Hall was designed by E.W.Mountford. Its foundation stone was laid by Alderman W.J.Clegg and it was officially opened by Queen Victoria on 21st May 1897.

It was faced with stone from Stoke Hall quarries. On the inside, Coxbench stone, which was suitable for fine carving, was used. The entrance hall was paved with marble On the roof are Westmoreland green slates and the turrets are oak with copper roofs. The tower reaches 180 feet in height, crowned by a copper case upon which poses the Roman god Vulcan.

At the foot of the grand staircase is a statue of the Duke of Norfolk, the city's first Lord Mayor.

In 1923, extensions in a similar Victorian Gothic style were opened by the Prince of Wales, later King Edward VIII.

From 1973-77, old buildings on Union Street and Norfolk Street were demolished to make way for the very modern 'egg-box' extension, connected to the older part by a first-floor footbridge. Only thirty years later, it was decided to demolish this building, and it should be gone by 2002.

Sheffield City Council's dignified, serious, no-nonsense demeanour cannot be compromised by frivolous talk of the supernatural. Staff are instructed not to talk about the ghostly man seen in the top-floor kitchen of the old building.

The Old Law Courts

Castle Street

I N THE ELEVENTH CENTURY English justice was administered locally, in shire and hundred courts for both criminal and civil cases and in manorial courts (held by lords of the manor for their tenants) for land disputes.

In the twelfth and thirteenth centuries, however, the local courts were stripped of most of their jurisdiction. Royal courts were established at Westminster administering 'Common Law' and judges were sent out around the country. At first, trial by jury was only for land disputes, but soon it became popular for criminal cases too. Coroners had (until 1977) the power to commit for trial in cases of suspicious death.

By the sixteenth century there were three Common Law Courts (Exchequer, Common Pleas and Kings Bench) and the Court of Chancery trying civil cases at Westminster Hall. For civil cases outside London there were the county Assizes, with judges sent from London. Matrimonial disputes, wills and intestacies were dealt with by the church courts. Manorial courts were often created Courts of Requests by Act of Parliament to try small claims.

Justices of the Peace date from the fourteenth century and became increasingly important. By 1600 they tried all petty crime and held preliminary examinations of more serious cases.

Each county and towns which were boroughs had a Quarter Sessions, which tried less serious cases by jury.

In 1846, county courts were established to try small civil claims. In 1857 jurisdiction of the church courts in matrimonial and probate suits was transferred to the new Courts of Divorce and Probate. In 1875 all existing superior courts were replaced by a High Court. In 1971 Assizes and Quarter Sessions were replaced by the Crown Court.

Sheffield grew around its castle. It was a manor with its own manorial court, which in the thirteenth century sat in the castle itself. Unlike the manorial court of Ecclesall, it was a court leet, trying both civil and criminal cases. Later it moved to Sembley Green (now the Wicker) and was nicknamed the Court of Sembly Quest or Assembly Inquest.

By the seventeenth century criminal cases were tried by the Justices of the

Peace for the West Riding in Sheffield town. From 1763, Rev. J. Wilkinson of Broomhall, Vicar of Sheffield, and from 1768, John Murray of Banner Cross were resident JP's. Wilkinson had a court room built onto his house. He also held court at the Cutlers' Hall. The JP's were so severe that their court-room was nicknamed 'Bang Beggars Hall'.

In 1700 a Town Hall was erected at the south-east corner of the Parish Churchyard. It contained prisoners' cells and was used for most of the eighteenth century as a court-house. By 1800, however, a room on the ground floor of the Cutlers' Hall in Church Street was being used. On court days prisoners stood in gangs in the churchyard and were taken across when their cases were called. Those sentenced to imprisonment or sent for trial at the West Riding Quarter Sessions went to the Wakefield House of Correction, chained together and on foot. Those sent for trial at the Assizes went to the county gaol at York.

In 1756, by Act of Parliament, the Sheffield and Ecclesall Courts of Requests had jurisdiction to try claims for sums of less than 40 shillings. The Sheffield debtors' prison was originally in Pudding Lane (now King Street) but in 1818 was moved to Scotland Street. The Ecclesall debtors' prison (known as Little Sheffield Gaol) was at the corner of Bishop Street and Tudor Street, near Moorfoot. In 1808 an Act gave these courts jurisdiction in cases concerning debts of up to £5 and also gave each jurisdiction over claims within each other's area, to prevent debtors escaping arrest by moving.

In 1808, the Town Trustees demolished the old Town Hall and built a new one in Castle Street (until December 1995 the Law Courts). It opened in 1810 and also served as a court-house for both the West Riding Magistrates and the Courts of Requests, and occasionally for adjourned sessions of the West Riding Quarter Sessions.

In 1888 Sheffield became a County Borough with a Borough Coroner. At this period inquests were often held in public houses. In 1876 the inquest into the Banner Cross murder by Charles Peace was held at the *Stag Inn*, Sharrow Head. This practice ended with the building of a public mortuary and coroner's court in Plum Street in 1884. It was replaced by a new building in Nursery Street in 1914 and in 1977 by the present Medico-Legal Centre in Watery Street.

In 1893 Sheffield (pop. 400,000) became a city, in 1905 it acquired a university, and in 1914 it was made a diocese. The fifth largest provincial city, it still had no Assize. (Liverpool had had an Assize since 1835 and Leeds and Manchester since 1865.) Finally it was granted an Assize in August 1940, but war prevented the building of a new court house in Eyre Street.

In 1953 Lord Chief Justice Goddard visited Castle Street and said that the court house would do as a temporary home for the Assizes. Alterations were carried out and Whirlow Court converted to serve as judges' lodgings.

The first Assize was opened on 23rd June 1955. In 1962 the Sheffield Assize Division became the separate judicial county of Hallamshire with its own High Sheriff.

From January 1st 1972, the Crown Court took over and in 1978 the Magistrates moved to a new court-house

nearby. In 1984-5 the County Court Hall in Bank Street (built in 1854) was given cells and courtrooms for criminal cases. The Castle Street building still proved inadequate. The Crown Court finally got its new building next to Police H.Q. in Snig Hill.

The Castle Street building is listed, so cannot be demolished.

A plain stone building erected in 1808, enlarged in 1833 at the expense of the Town Trustees, who in 1866 leased it to the Corporation for 500 years for a nominal rent, it was remodelled in 1878 with further extensions in 1896. It is connected with the city police offices (the old police H.Q. from 1866) in Castle Green by underground passages.

In Court 2 – originally Court 1 – an electrician and a court official froze with terror when a lamp suddenly started swinging by itself. Other people had the same experience at different times. Charles Peace is said to haunt his old cell. Anyone sitting in a chair placed on the site where his bed was, will fall asleep.

Castle Street used to be called Truelove's Gutter, because a Mr Truelove owned property there. An open gutter ran down the middle of the street, which was periodically cleansed by water released from Barker's Pool, a small reservoir built in 1434 by Mr Barker of Balm Green. A gibbet stood at the crossroads with Waingate, so that the ghosts of malefactors did not know which way to go and remained to haunt the area.

The Brown Bear

109 Norfolk Street
....

THE BUILDING is about two hundred years old and was built on the site of Sheffield 's first public library, which was opened in 1771 by Thomas Saunders and his daughter, Esther Caterer. It is first recorded in the directory of 1876 as the *Brown Bear* with George Beet as victualler.

The license appears to have been transferred from lower down the street. In 1839 at No.71 John Wild kept the *Brown Bear* as well as carrying on his trade as a manufacturer of table knives, scissors, razors, shoe-knives, etc. From 1841, the *Brown Bear* had moved to No.75 with Martha Wild as victualler. From 1845, the license at No.75 was in the name of John Wild. Then in 1852 Martha Wild was again in charge. However from 1854 to 1856 John Towroe was victualler and from 1859 to 1868 John Darley. It was in 1876 when Charles Smith and Sons, ironmongers, took over the whole site of Nos. 71-5 that the *Brown Bear* moved to No.109.

Beer used to be brewed on the premises, but the huge vat at the back is now locked up. It was beside the vat that a customer saw the shadowy figure of a man.

The ghost is said to be that of a man, who had been injured in a coach accident. His wife took a lover. While waiting for her to come home from seeing her lover, he hung himself. He still paces up and down waiting for her. There is a definite air of sadness upstairs. John Conroy, later at the *Three Tuns*, was relief manager at the *Brown Bear* in 1985. He was on the top floor alone late at night doing the tills, when the room went cold and he could hardly get his breath as he heard footsteps coming across the bare floorboards towards him. He was so terrified that he shoved the money into the safe without counting it and ran downstairs, out of the pub, locking the door but forgetting to set the alarm in his haste. The following morning the cleaners, waiting for him to open up, noticed his still nervous state. They asked, 'Did you see the ghost, then?'

A previous landlord is said to have been driven crazy. He used to stalk around the pub dressed in a cowboy hat with a revolver in each hand, ready to shoot the ghost.

Queen's Hotel
85 Scotland Street

....

O PENED IN 1797, the *Queen's* finally closed down on Sunday February 23rd, 1997.

A favourite rendezvous for actors and the gay community, it was famed as Sheffield's wackiest hotel, where many a wild party was held.

It was owned by Wards and the manager since 1993 was David Ward with the assistance of his partner, Jim.

The pub had a ghostly organist.

Janet Bond, who took over the license in January 1989, experienced a sudden drop in temperature after midnight and on one occasion a glass was thrown into the air and smashed on the floor.

It was in June that the organist took to waking Janet and her daughter, Jane. They did not recognise the tune that was being played but at least once a week the recital began about midnight.

Their living organist complained about people tampering with the organ. Janet tried to assure him that no-one had been

near it. However she did not intend to call in a priest to exorcise the spirit, her motto being 'Live and let live.'

Old Queen's Head

Pond Street

···

TUCKED AWAY beside Pond Street Bus Station, dwarfed by modern buildings, lies the oldest house in the city. Several times it has been threatened with demolition by the council, who have wanted to use the land for redevelopment, but as a listed building in good repair it is hopefully saved for ever.

Parts of it date back to 1400 AD and it was probably the lodge of Sheffield Castle to which it is connected by tunnels, now blocked up. It was used for fishing expeditions to the nearby ponds, hence its original name, 'The Hawle in the Ponds'. According to William Fairbank's 1771 plan of Sheffield, Pond Hill was then Pond Well Hill. Mary Queen of Scots is said to have walked along the connecting tunnel from the unhealthy Sheffield Castle, where she was imprisoned, to take the fresher air by the ponds. Her shoulder cape was found in the tunnel many years ago.

It is possible that with the demolition of the Castle by Cromwell and its being rented by tenants, the status of the lodge declined and the ducal washing was done there up to 1706, when the Manor House was abandoned by the eighth Duke of Norfolk. When the records of the Sheffield Licensing Magistrates began in 1872 it was already a beer-house and indeed it was known to be such as far back as 1841. The Corporation bought it from Tennant Brothers Ltd in 1935 but, not being allowed to demolish it, leased it to John Smith's brewery.

From January 1980 the landlord was Mr Couldwell. The relief circuit manager before him said that the cleaners refused to clean the Snug because one of them, called Mary, had seen a little old man with two jugs in his hands standing by the fireplace, which is original and dates from 1400.

Mr Couldwell's cleaners preferred to clean the vast cellars rather than the Snug, although no-one else had seen the old man. There were however indications that he was still around. The top bolt on the door of the snug was frequently found to have unfastened itself overnight, and on one occasion, in the middle of the night, Mrs Couldwell told her husband that she was sure there was someone in the pub. He went downstairs to investigate, but found no-one. However as he went back upstairs again, he heard footsteps below.

Mr Couldwell's sister-in-law saw a figure in the hall after closing time.

From April 1985, the manager was Joe Butler. His two cats refused to go near the Snug and the only cleaner who would work there, Audrey, always shouted 'Good Morning!' before she went in, to give the ghosts a chance to disappear.

Mr Butler turned off the pumps every night, but in the morning he would find them back on. Lights in the cellar would switch themselves on and off and he was often left in complete darkness down there. He often felt as though something cold had passed him and he shivered. The barman Mark's wife, Shelley, had the same feeling. Mark himself was trying to solve the biggest mystery, of a half-pint of beer left every night on the same beer mat at a certain table. He had not seen anyone buying it or sitting there and it was never touched.

Like Mr Couldwell, he would bolt the Snug door each night and frequently found it wide open in the morning.

In December 1990, Lisa, who owned it for four years, having previously been relief manageress, described how she and the barmaid, Nicola slept in the two attic bedrooms. On more than one occasion Lisa's clothes disappeared from the foot of the bed, where she had left them, as she saw when she woke up in the morning. Yet the next night, when she went upstairs, they had been returned to the foot of the bed. In the meantime she had searched everywhere.

Once, when Nicola was in the cellar, a heavy cupboard, which was ordinarily difficult to move, moved across the floor twice by itself. She came upstairs terrified and refused to go down again.

The pub was bought by the Tom Cobleigh Company in 1993. They completely renovated it, adding a kitchen with a dining-room upstairs. The wall separating the Snug from the lounge has been removed.

While the building work was going on, a little old man in a flat cap was seen several times in various parts of the old building. He has never yet ventured into the new kitchen extension in the lounge and upstairs. Eloise Barker and her husband, Ben McLellan felt an icy presence in the lounge and upstairs.

Marples' Hotel

Fitzalan Square

....

ON THE NIGHT OF 12th December 1940, during the Sheffield Blitz, the old *Marples' Hotel* received a direct hit. A dance was being held and the hotel was crowded. There were only seven survivors. Sixty-four bodies were finally identified, but there were fragments of six more. Such a disaster gave rise to many stories. It was said that many of the people had survived the blast as they had taken refuge in the cellars, but before they could be freed from their tomb by rescue workers, they were overcome by the fumes from the alcohol stored there. It was also said that when the new *Marples' Hotel* was finally built in 1958-59, more skeletons were found.

Whatever the truth about the tragedy, in the post-war years, on each anniversary of the bombing, Sheffielders placed wreaths on the rubble.

The *Marples' Hotel* was originally called the Market Street Wine Vaults. In 1876 there was a Wine and Spirit Commercial Hotel, also known as the Old London Mart at No.64 High Street on the corner with what was then Market Street. In 1888 the owner, Mr Atley, sold the seven-storey building to Mr John Marples for £6,000. Edward Marples became its licensee and it became the Market Street Wine Vaults. Sheffielders started calling it *The Marples*, but it only officially became so in 1959 when the new hotel was built.

A visitor to the city, who did not know the history of the hotel, has said that as she walked by the new *Marples*, she smelled the heavy, sickly scent of flowers!

The Hogshead

Orchard Street

························

K NOWN AS *The Museum* for most of its life, this old pub was re-named the *Orchard* at the time of the opening of Orchard Square in 1987.

In March 1993 it was refurbished to become the *Hogshead*, with the pub entrance still in Orchard Street, but with a sandwich shop at the rear, with an entrance onto the square.

Today, no-one would guess that this cosy inn used to be the mortuary for the old Medical School opposite. There is no chilly or spooky atmosphere. Ernest Bray, the landlord in the 1980s was sure that there was a ghost. Like his predecessor, Peter Dickinson, he had the experience of finding even full gas bottles, used for introducing bubbles into beer, turned off. The ghost, like several other pub ghosts around Sheffield, clearly preferred traditional beer, in keeping with its surroundings. Since real ale was re-introduced in 1979, the ghost became less active, but still showed his disapproval of lager. Nothing has happened lately.

The Market Tavern

27 Exchange Street

·································

B EHIND Castle Market is to be found a building well-known in Sheffield history. A Berni Inn from August 1969 and from June 1984 owned by Mecca as the Garden Restaurant, it has always been better known as *The Old Number Twelve*.

Its most famous landlord was Thomas Wiley, son of Robert Wiley, a mercer at the upper corner of Change Alley and Market Place. Thomas quarrelled with his father and instead of a mercer became a licensed victualler. In 1828 he was noted as being the landlord of the *Theatre Tavern*, Arundel Steet, but early in 1832 he had moved to No.12 Old Haymarket, where he was to prove very enterprising.

Mr Murdo Young, proprietor of the *Sun* newspaper had begun to publish late editions giving the Parliamentary debates up to post time. Young sent the papers by express to the main towns of England. Wiley became his Sheffield agent. When the Reform Bill was passed on 5th June 1832 Wiley reached Sheffield with the news at 12.30noon, having travelled by horse in 12 hours. Wiley's window became the resort of all anxious for the latest news, and Wiley became one of the most popular men in town.

On 14th December 1832, soldiers of an Irish regiment, drawn up in the gateway of the great *Tontine* coaching inn opposite, fired at a crowd gathered on the night of the first Sheffield election, killing five people and wounding others. A bullet went through the woodwork in the lower part of the window of No.12. Wiley had the hole carefully preserved and the date painted around it.

The house was then called the *Sun*, though whether because of its connection with the newspaper or because that had been the name of a pub on the site over a hundred years before, is not known.

It is not known whether Wiley's *Sun* occupied the original building or whether it was rebuilt sometime before 1839. It was called the *Sun* still in 1837, but a few years later it had become the *Old No.12*, Thomas Wiley being described as a wine and spirit merchant.

At the first municipal election Wiley was returned as one of the members for St. Peter's Ward. In November 1849 he was elected alderman. The previous March, the freeholders had elected him a member of the Town Trust, and in April the townsmen had presented him with a 200 guinea silver-plated dinner service. Every Christmas he presented food and blankets to old people.

Thomas Wiley died of a heart attack on 14th October 1851, aged 57, and was buried at St. John's Church, with the mayor and corporation in attendance.

An advertisement for 1849 described Wiley's at the Old No.12 as agents for wholesale and retail, foreign and British wine and spirit, vaults and stores. After his death the firm became Wiley and Co. Ltd, by 1924 being found at 23 and 25 The Haymarket

At one time between the two World Wars, the *Old No.12* was known as *The Old Rotherham House*. There is supposed to be a tunnel from it to the Castle. Roy Bell, a porter when it was the Berni Inn, described how it was when the downstairs restaurant was used as a concert room, where artists such as Bobby Knutt performed.

The ghost is said to be Charlie, an old customer, who was a miner. In the bad old days when children still worked in the mines, a young boy was trapped. Charlie went in to rescue him and was also killed.

A woman customer was seated in the Variety Bar upstairs, and out of the corner of her eye saw a shadow beside her which was gone as she turned her head. Glasses were seen to move by themselves.

One Saturday night, Mr Bell saw the door to the cellar, at the side of the bar downstairs, open and a shadow walk out through the main door and back again. Several people have seen the shadow and there is an eerie atmosphere in the cellar.

Charlie also has the unnerving habit of sighing. A cleaning lady told how she was in the upstairs restaurant when she heard a deep, sorrowful sigh behind her.

Unfortunately, when the building became the Garden Restaurant there were considerable alterations. The wall dividing the concert room from the rest of the ground floor was partly removed and the atmosphere and decor of the entire place had an ultra-modern liveliness, which, though attractive in its own way, appealed more to a younger clientele than the comfortable gentility of the Berni Inn, which suited a ghost of Charlie's generation.

As the *Market Tavern* it has been redecorated to restore the Victorian atmosphere but the ghost has not been seen upstairs recently.

The cellars remain much the same, so perhaps he still lives there, now too nervous to show himself as he tries to adjust to the modern age.

The Corporation
9-39 Bank Street
....

THERE IS AN interesting legend concerning this well-known night-club and restaurant. The ghost of a man sits among the diners. He used to meet his sweetheart at a café which stood on the site. She was killed when it was bombed during the Second World Ward, but he is still waiting for her. A romantic story.

Unfortunately, the old directories have no record of a café on the site of numbers 9-39. Since the First World War the occupants of the old block of offices were accountants, solicitors and such-like dignatories. However, the *George and Dragon* pub stood at No.39 at the corner of Meeting House Lane and Bank Street. It was closed down between 1916 and 1919, during the First World War, when it became an auctioneers.

Did the ghostly diner meet his sweetheart in the pub? A further snag to the legend is that the buildings survived the Second World War. Among other occupants in, for instance, 1951 we find the Probation Offices at No.39 and the office of the Clerk of the Peace at No.25.

From 1959 we find only Sintaloy Products Ltd., tool manufacturers and the Empire Window Cleaning Service at No.39a on the site, right up to Meeting House Lane. In 1961 only the window cleaners remained. By 1963 they too had gone, as the buildings were demolished.

Then, in 1968, Martins Bank and the Cavendish Club appear at No.9 and Ashington and Denton, solicitors at No.25. In 1971 *Bailey's* night club had taken over the whole block. In 1977 it became *Romeo and Juliets*, in 1986 *Cairo Jax*, *Cairo's* for short.

Despite the garbled history of the legend, one fact is undisputable. There is a ghost in the night club and he was a habitue of Bailey's as well as Romeo and Juliet's.

The cleaning ladies of Bailey's were so used to him that they used to just vacuum around him. He would also stand outside asking directions of passers-by, who, even if they did not realise he was a ghost, may have been puzzled by his 1930s clothes. At Romeo and Juliet's he has been seen in a certain corridor, and a bar lady saw him seated in a corner after the other customers had gone. Not realising who he was, she told him that they were closed and he should not be there. She turned away for an instant. When she looked back, he was gone.

In the 1960s he was known as Mr Fox and reputedly told a spiritualist he was looking for the shop with three bullseye panes of glass in one window.

Around 1970 David Holmes was visiting the Cavendish Club with his wife and another couple. They were seated in the lounge, waiting for the star turn, Norman Wisdom, just before the lights went down. Mr Holmes glanced idly around the room. The main entrance to the room was behind the bar area and a partition blocked off the view to the door. As he looked a lady walked around the partition and down the steps into the main bar area. She was the perfect 'Crinoline Lady', carrying a rolled up parasol and wearing a large hat, tight bodice and an enormous flowing skirt.

He glanced back to tell his wife and friends, but when he turned around the lady disappeared before his eyes. He tried to explain what he had seen, but everyone laughed and thought he was playing a joke on them. Then Norman Wisdom came on and the 'ghost' was forgotten by everyone but Mr Holmes.

An article in *The Star* about the same time told of other people seeing the 'Crinoline Lady'. *Cairo's* is now called *The Corporation*.

The Three Tuns

39-41 Silver Street Head
....

I N THE MIDDLE of the last century Silver Street Head was well-endowed with pubs and beer retailers – the *Union Inn*, the *Earl Grey*, *Reform* and the *Punch Bowl* to name but a few. In 1839 Samuel Bishop was the landlord at No.39, the *Old Three Tuns*. In 1845 when J.C.Ragg was landlord the name was shortened to the *Three Tuns*, which originated in the coat of arms of the Vintners' Company.

There was a pub on the site before 1745, when Richard Staniforth was victualler, but the first building was recorded in 1513, when it was a washhouse for a nearby nunnery, St. Vincent's Convent. It continued as such until the Civil War. A priest-hole was found beneath the present bar, but it is now bricked up.

The building is triangular-shaped and in a false room on the corner the date '1802' was discovered on the wall during recent renovations. Presumably the present building dates from then, but the staircase and foundations are from the early eighteenth century. The old walls in the cellars were

constructed with horsehair. Victorian sewers run through the cellars below the new sewers. Nearby used to be Reek Croft, where there was an open sewer or reek.

Until it was bought by Tetleys and incorporated into the pub in 1987, No.41 was a chandlers and at one time a silver-smiths.

Until the summer of 1997, the landlord was David John Conroy. Since 1987 he three times heard a woman sobbing in the cellar. Glasses disappeared down there and the taps turned themselves off. Cats and dogs refusd to go into the cellar. An old landlady, terrified after seeing a nun there, refused to go down again. A previous land-lady's mother had to go into a home, because she was too scared to live at the pub after she saw the nun in the bar.

In 1988, Fiona, a training officer with Tetleys, had a nasty experience in the cellar, which she would not talk about.

Roxy's, Arundel Gate

(formerly Top Rank)

T HE WELL-KNOWN night club is the setting for several spooky incidents. The mechanical lights, which spin round, were known to come on by themselves. In the balcony upstairs ashtrays flew around. Internal telephones rang when no-one was on the line.

Bar No.1 was Barry Noble's bar. When he died, his youngest son took over. Two American lads used to work there and stood on the same spot as Barry. The night lad, Simon, would pat the girls on their behinds. One night Joyce felt someone pat her, but Simon was not there. The bar doors flapped, opening and shutting. The staff felt that it was Barry objecting to any-one else standing in his place.

In 1999 the building was leased to St. Thomas' Church and is due to be replaced by a 169-room hotel and retail units at some future date.

Paradise Square

P ARADISE SQUARE was built on the site of a cornfield, called Hick's Stile Field.

In 1832 Joseph Woolhouse told how his grandfather, who lived at Green Lane, kept a public house and also made pocket knives. One of his men was lame and for many years dependent on crutches. He was out late one evening and was walking along Campo Lane, to reach his home in Gregory Row, which was a very narrow street at the bottom of Hick's Stile Field, when he saw coming towards him a barghast, a large black dog with luminous eyes and long, sharp teeth (usually found in towns close to stiles and gateways). He managed to get over the stile into the field, but to his hor-ror the barghast followed him and was gaining on him. Faster and faster he went until in the middle of the field he dropped his crutches and 'away he went without them, and never stopt or look'd behind him until he got home'. His wife had fastened the door, but he was too terrified to wait for her to open it and burst it open. He told her about the barghast outside, but she was more frightened at him coming home without his crutches. When daylight came he ventured out to look for his crutches and found them where he had dropped them. When he went to work, his mates were nearly as frightened as his wife at seeing him without his crutches but were quick to help him celebrate with some ale. He lived on for many years and never needed his crutches again.

In 1736 Thomas Broadbent leased the field from the Wade family and built a row of houses at the top. He had five daughters and made sure of marrying them off by offering a house to any would-be husbands. Paradise Square used to be called Pot Square, from the many traders who set out their pots for sale on the cobbles. The Sheffield Statute Hirings Fair was held there on St. Simon and St. Jude's Feast, October 28th, when folk offered themselves for hire. Even wives could be bought at the market. In 1796 John Lees, a steel burner brought his wife with a horse's halter around her neck to be auctioned off. Samuel Hill bought her for sixpence! By 1822 either the cost of living had gone up or a certain hatter's wife was prettier. He sold her for five shillings and a gold watch!

The Anglo-Palladian architecture of the buildings around the square is based on the classical styles of Greece and Rome. They are now mainly occupied by solicitors, but in their day have seen some famous (or infamous) faces. When Francis Chantrey finished his apprenticeship with Mr R. Ramsey, the print seller on High Street he moved to 24 Paradise Square, where he set up as a portrait painter until he moved to London in 1802, yet keeping a house on Norfolk Row.

The Square was regularly used for public meetings. In September 1838 20,000 people are said to have gathered there for a

Chartist rally. On the north side is a balcony from which John Wesley (1703-91) used to address his open-air congregations.

Charles Peace (hanged in.1879) used to attend Hebblethwaite's Academy, later the Middle Class School, at No's.18 and 20, which closed in 1937.

In 1852 there were 1,622 arrests for drunkeness in Sheffield and local directories for 1856 show at least 11 beerhouses in the Crofts area with its insanitary back-to-back houses. The Q in the Corner (later the Shrewsbury was in the Square itself and there the famous fiddler, Blind Stephen, who had only to hear a tune once to be able to play it, would talk with his friends about the ghosts in the churchyard, later the Cathedral yard.

The Fire Museum

West Bar Green

THIS USED TO BE a combined fire station and police station, until it was replaced by the Fire Station on Division Street, (which was itself replaced in the 1980s by a modern building on Wellington Street).

In 1350 the only fire equipment in the town was a number of leather buckets hanging on pegs in the old Town Hall near the Parish Church and in the Parish

Council chancel, rather useless considering that most of the buildings then were built of timber with thatched roofs. However they were each surrounded by their own gardens, which would have helped stop the spread of a fire to neighbouring properties.

Barker's Pool was built in 1434 to store spring water from the hill above West Bar, which could be used to fight fires. The Burgess Accounts of 1620 include an annual fee of 1s-6d paid to Thomas Wheelwright for the maintenance of leather buckets.

The Great Fire of London in 1666 must have horrified the Burgesses of Sheffield, but it was not until 1703 that they could bring themselves to delve into their pockets to buy the town's first fire engine – a handcart with a pump operated by large handles. It cost the Town Trustees a shilling every time it was filled with water.

At first it was kept at the Parish Church, then in 1714 its own garage was built, costing £22-12s-9d. In 1784 the town splashed out on a more efficient fire engine, made by Hadley & Sons for £45-17s.

In 1807 Insurance Fire Brigades were established. A householder paid a premium to the brigade and was given a large metal plaque to fix onto the building. In case of fire the owner would send a messenger to the Insurance Office, who would send out their brigade. If uninsured premises were on fire, the brigade would go if the owner agreed to pay a charge.

The town's fire engine was given to the Birmingham Fire Insurance Office, which undertook to maintain the equipment and pay the firemen's wages in return for having all the town's insurance. In 1808 a Sheffield Fire Office was opened in George Street. They kept a fire engine and escape ladder at the Town Hall. Other fire offices were opened by various insurance companies. To be on the safe side, people would insure with more than one company.

In 1869 the Council took over the Fire Services. It was agreed that the insurance companies would present all their engines to the town and pay a joint contribution towards the cost of the service. The first fire station was in Norfolk Street with John Pound as Superintendant. He formed a brigade with fifteen young police constables.

In 1870 the Council leased 17 houses in Hill Street and Balm Green for the firemen, and electric bells were installed in each. The engines and escape ladders were moved to a new fire station in Barker's Pool. Anyone wanting the brigade at night would knock on a metal plate set into the wall to awaken the caretaker, who would turn out the horses and engines ready for the firemen.

In 1874 water hose carts were housed at four divisional police stations. In 1876 Sheffield obtained a steam-operated engine and in 1883 a new station was built in Rockingham Street. By 1895 the town had three horse-drawn steam engines and five fire escapes. One four-wheeled tender with escape ladders was pulled by five horses.

In 1900 a larger, better equipped fire station, built by Messrs. Ash, Son and Biggin was opened at West Bar. It was combined with a police station, which was on the left-hand side of the building. The horses were stabled behind the engine, so they were able to turn out much quicker. From 1903 they had a horse-drawn turntable fire escape worked by compressed carbon dioxide. From 1907 they had motor-driven fire engines and by 1911 breathing apparatus.

When the First World War broke out, many of the forty Sheffield firemen volunteered to fight, so the fire service had problems with manpower. In 1919 they were back to normal with four officers and thirty-nine men and fully motorised.

During the Second World War with its terrible air raids the National Fire Service was formed and the Sheffield Police Fire Brigade was disbanded after 72 years service. On April 1st 1948 responsibility for fire-fighting reverted to the local authorities and the Sheffield Fire Brigade was separated from the police. It is now called the South Yorkshire County Fire and Rescue Service.

In 1929, a new fire-station was opened in Division Street and the old one at West Bar was henceforth only used as a police station, being the Central Division H.Q. and later from 1951 H.Q for 'B' Division and also the Mechanical Transport Department. From 1957 it was in 'F' Division. According to *Kelly's Directory* for 1965 it was then empty.

Happily, by 1968 it was occupied by Paradise House Ltd. The following year Group 4 Total Security and Portland Autos (Sheffield) Ltd were in occupation, but it was again empty in 1970. From 1971 to at least 1974 Harrison (Office Supplies) Co was using it as a warehouse, when it was called Peter House.

When the firemen of the South Yorkshire Fire Service Historical Society took it over in 1984 it had been derelict for several years. They renovated the building, spending £26,000 just on the roof. The South Yorkshire Fire Service Museum opened in 1986 with exhibits dating back to 1794. As a registered educational charity it is opened by special arrangement during the week to parties of school children and others, but is open to the general public only on Sundays. Visitors can see the police cells, the old stables, the old fire engines and an array of equipment, medals, photographs and records. If they are lucky , they will see a fireman sliding down the pole. The museum is funded by the proceeds from the souvenir shop and entrance fees. It is run by volunteers and well worth a visit.

The museum has been haunted since the early nineteen-eighties by a man in a sailor-type uniform with a square-cut collar, lanyard and whistle. Early firemen's uniforms were modelled on naval uniforms. He has been seen by different people at different times and seems peaceable and friendly. Psychics have detected the presence of seven ghosts on the top floor. They said that they are of former wardens and gave five names of men who worked there between 1903 and 1992. Tony Hunter from the museum checked the records and found three of the names.

Old Britannia Music Hall

111-115 West Bar
....

SHEFFIELD had more music halls and theatres than any other provincial town in the last century, many smaller halls being attached to public houses. The building which later housed the *Britannia Music Hall* was built between 1796 and 1800, originally for shops, onto the *Tankard Tavern* in a heavily populated industrial area.

The *Old Tankard Music Hall* opened in the late 1850s or early 1860s and was later re-named the Britannia Music Hall.

At first, the working-class patrons paid 3d and were given a pint of beer on entering. It was a 'posh' hall and later, as the *Britannia*, charged 6d while other halls charged 3d. The audience would throw half-pennies at acts they didn't like, sometimes cutting open the artiste's hand or even head.

The artistes were the proprietor and his family, with a pianist, violinist and local people who might appear at two halls on the same night. Dan Leno, the comedian, appeared at the *Britannia* as a boy dancing a clog dance. (His father ran Leno's Varieties on the site of the later *Lyceum Theatre*.)

The opening of the *Empire Palace of Varieties,* on 4th November 1895, coincided with new and stricter safety laws.

Several small music halls, including the *Britannia*, had to close in 1896-7.

Messrs. William Green and Co. took over the premises in 1906 for their stove and fireplace showrooms. For over sixty years they tried to preserve as much as possible of the old features, and indeed used the old stage as a loading bay. However, after H.R. Wholesalers used it as their warehouse it remained empty for several years and the whole building was allowed to deteriorate badly. Fortunately, in April 1982 Mr Philip Knowles bought it to house his Pink Champagne Wedding Centre, and gradually restored it.

The Music Hall held about a thousand spectators. Some sat around small tables on the same level as the stage, on the first floor. The poorer folk sat on wooden step seats upstairs. Green's installed toilets here, keeping the original floor under the new. The 170-foot high building was solidly built with one-and-a-quarter-inch thick girders and royal oak beams. The pulleys for the trapezes still remained.

The shop assistants saw the ghost frequently and were never afraid of her. Since the pink Champagne Wedding Centre opened, Mr Philip Knowles was at first the only one to see her, firstly only faintly on the third floor near the toilets and by the screens on the stage level. With each appearance, however, her image gradually became clearer.

He talked to her, hoping that as she came to trust him more, she would answer him. She was beautiful, with shoulder-length gold-brown hair in ringlets. She wore the drab dress of an Edwardian working-class girl and was about twenty-six years old. There was a warm aura about her.

Surely she was not responsible for the alarming happening just before Christmas 1984? Mr Knowles was alone in the building at closing time about six o'clock, collecting his account books on the ground floor office. Footsteps upstairs did not bother him. He was used to them by now. Suddenly there was a thunderous noise, which he described as like a herd of horses. Could it have been the audience gathering upstairs in the Music Hall?

Mr Knowles did not stop to investigate. He flew out of the shop, jumped into his car and drove home like a mad man, arriving there white in the face, as his wife testified.

Some weeks later, two women were working late on a wedding dress required for the following day. One of them went upstairs and saw the ghost. Pulling herself together, she went back down, not telling the other woman. A little time later the other assistant went up and saw the ghost too. She did not have such strong nerves. Her panic communicated itself to her companion and they both rushed off to West Bar police station.

Officers with dogs accompanied them back to the shop, but they could not persuade the dogs, who were clearly terrified, to go upstairs.

Not long after the Wedding Centre closed down and the Music Hall was once more left to ghosts and vandals. In May 1987 it re-opened as Harmony Wedding World, under new management.

After again being empty for a long while, the old *Britannia* was taken over by Door World. During April 1992 a fire swept through the business premises fronting the building. Conservationists said that the music hall should be rebuilt but Door World is now a car park owned by Bentleys. Have the homeless ghosts of the old music hall – one of only six of its type remaining in the country – moved into the Fire Museum next door?

The front of the site of the old *Brittania Music Hall* is now occupied by the West Bar Motor Company.

Don Picture House

West Bar

···

THE CINEMA OPENED ON 18th November 1912 with a seating capacity of 950. It had a large orchestra. In May 1957 a very large screen was installed, together with the latest sound equipment, yet it closed down on 1st March 1958.

Designed by the architect H.L. Paterson, its proprietors were the Don Picture Palace Co. Ltd., controlled from 1927 by Sheffield and District Cinematograph Theatres Ltd. It was subsequently used as a showroom for the Bradford Woollen Company before it was taken over by E.L.S. Did this upset the ghost who only appeared afterwards?

Swing doors at the top of the building open and close of their own accord and mysterious noises have been heard. In April 1979 there was a fire, which badly damaged the warehouse section, previously the old projection room. One of the men re-decorating, who had never heard of the ghost, saw a figure of a man go into the toilets ahead of him, but when he himself entered there was no-one there. The ghost also whispers the names of members of staff. A section manager has three times heard his name whispered, when he knew that he was alone in the building.

Jeffrey Beardow, who was the junior projectionist at the cinema, went back on a visit and heard the whirring sounds of the projector even though the room was empty. He is certain that the ghost is that of the chief projectionist, the eccentric Mr Potter. With the cinema since its opening, he had devoted his life to it. He cycled every day, whatever the weather, from his home in the Ecclesall area. He never used the tram-car, but had not missed a day even during the Blitz. He kept his bicycle in the projection room. Descriptions of the ghost fit him.

He always wore plus-fours and a tweed jacket protected by a brown or grey overall. The ghost wears overalls. Mr Beardow said that Mr Potter used to creep into the projection room and whisper his name in order to make him jump. No doubt old Mr Potter was upset to see his beloved cinema turned into a furniture store!

The building's occupant for several years was Titan Discount Superstore. It is now refurbished and occupied by Safestore.

The Old Gas Showrooms

73 The Moor

···

NO.73 THE MOOR, at the corner of Earl Street, has had a chequered history. Before World War II it was Weaver to Wearer Ltd, tailors, who remained there after the war at Nos.73 and 75. Jay's Furnishing Stores were at Nos. 69-73 from 1962-5. They were followed by Cavendish Furnishing Stores. The longest recent occupant was British Gas, who used it for offices and showrooms. An auto accessory company preceded the Publishers Book Clearance and Discount Book Stores, famous for selling books by weight, who were there for two years until the end of February 2000. It was staff at the bookshop, who reported the presence, on the first floor, of the shop's permanent resident, a man who whistles. It is now divided into two shops, House Works and, on the corner, Price Pounder.

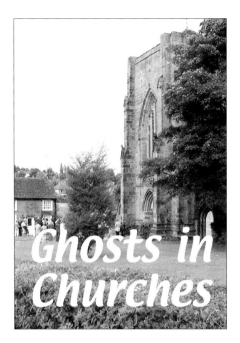

Ecclesfield Parish Church

St. Mary the Virgin, Church Street

··

LTHOUGH THERE IS no mention of a church at 'Eclesfelt', the manor held by Roger de Busli, according to the Domesday Book, the very name, derived from the Latin 'ecclesia', 'a church', and the Teutonic 'feld', 'open country' implies that the Anglo-Saxon invaders found a British church there, probably between 625 and 650 AD, though not necessarily on the same site as the present church. It may have been in ruins at the time of the Domesday survey, because Earl Waltheof, the lord of Hallam and husband of William the Conqueror's niece, Judith, took part in the 1069 rebellion and William laid waste much of Yorkshire in reprisal. Waltheof was executed in 1076 after a second rebellion, but Judith retained her lands. It was either she or Roger de Lovetot who donated Ecclesfield church to the Abbey of

St Wandrille, near Rouen in Normandy.

An eleventh-century cross shaft was dug up from the churchyard in the 19th century. Otherwise the Norman remains consist of some circular columns on the north side of the nave, not necessarily in their original positions, and the keeled responds or half-pillars at the west end. In the fourteenth century some re-building was done, but, at a time of economic stagnation and the horrors of the Black Death, not completed. Most of the church dates from the fifteenth century. Ecclesfield church had dependant chapels at Sheffield, Bradfield and Whiston. Bradfield and Aldwark remained in Ecclesfield parish until the 19th century. Sheffield became a separate parish in the 14th century.

In 1385, when Richard II dissolved alien priories, he gave Ecclesfield church to the Carthusian monastery of St Anne near Coventry, and the lands were leased to local farmers. In 1536-40, at the dissolution of the monasteries, the lands and buildings passed into secular hands for good.

There is a legend that a black-robed monk walks up to the church and into it straight through the solid wall, probably at a spot where there used to be a door. However, he has not been seen in recent years. The priory adjacent to the church, built or rebuilt in 1270, is also reputed to be haunted. However, the churchwarden who lives there has not yet seen anything.

St. Mary's Parish Church

Handsworth Road

··

HE FIRST PARISH CHURCH of Handsworth was built before 1171 either by William de Lovetot or his father, Richard. It was a small Norman building with a short chancel. St. Katherine's Chapel was added during the first half of the thirteenth century and has always been associated with Maud de Lovetot. On her marriage to Gerard de Furnival, her great estates in Sheffield and the counties of York and Nottingham were transferred to the Furnival family who held them, until the male line ended a hundred and eighty years later, as Lords of Hallamshire. When Gerard went off on the Sixth Crusade, Maud prayed in vain for him in the chapel. He died at Jerusalem in 1219. The chapel may originally have been a chantry as it had oblations, a holy water stoop and a door of its own. The Rectory on the south side of the church was originally built in the first half of the thirteenth century.

The church has a ghost. The verger has twice seen a lady in grey, dressed rather like a nun, standing by the font in the twilight. A cleaner has also seen her twice. One theory is that she is Grysill, wife of the first rector of St. Mary's. She bore seven children, dying as she gave birth to the twins. For some reason, many years ago, the inscribed slab over her tomb was moved from the nave to St Margaret's Chapel. Was her rest disturbed?

Parish Church of St. James

Norton
....

THE PARISH CHURCH dates from Saxon times. It was bestowed upon Beauchief Abbey between 1172 and 1176 by Robert FitzRanulf, Lord of Norton, Marnham and Alfreton. The interior is a mixture of late Norman and Early English styles. The tower arch dates from about 1180. The Blythe chapel, with the tombs of the Blythe family of Bishops' House, was constructed in 1520. There are monuments to such old Norton families as the Shores of Norton Hall and the Bagshawes

of Oakes Park.

The carved salamander with wings and long ears on the Early English font is said to represent the Devil witnessing with disgust each child being Baptised into Christianity. The old peal of six bells was re-cast and two new bells added in 1896 as a memorial to F.W. Bagshawe, Esq.

In 1882, when the church was restored, the roofs were re-covered with lead, the galleries removed, the pews replaced by benches, the floor re-paved, some stained glass windows put in and an organ chamber constructed.

The grave of Sir Francis Chantrey, the famous sculptor (1781-1841), who was born in Norton, is just outside the porch, and an obelisk monument to him was erected in 1854 on the remains of the ancient village green nearby. There is a legend that a ghost walks in the churchyard. Some say that it is of a lady whose murdered body was dumped in the churchyard in January 1947. However, as the lady in question was discovered in a lane by St. Paul's, Norton Lees, this is clearly a case of mistaken identity. A more romantic story is that the ghost is of a crusader who was killed in the Holy Land and whose decapitated body was returned and buried in his native village. The journey home must have taken weeks, and in order that his body should arrive in a good state of preservation (perhaps pickled or salted in those days before refrigeration) his viscera was removed.

Unfortunately, by a careless oversight, they were not sent with him. So, it is said, the poor knight is still searching for his innards! He may also have been searching inside the church.

In 1940, however, the parish clerk and his apprentice were practising on the organ, in the west gallery at dusk, when they realised they were being watched by a ghostly woman seated in a pew. They rushed out and never played the organ at dusk again.

A legend tells of a tunnel between Beauchief Abbey and Norton St. James'. A treasure chest halfway along can only be brought away on a white horse, which must be shod the wrong way round and must approach the chest backwards, while the chest must be fastened behind its head.

Old Quaker's Burial Ground and Underbank Chapel

Stannington

ADJACENT TO the old turnpike, just outside Stannington on the road to Moscar, there is still the remains of the burial ground in a clump of trees surrounded by a wall, now called Bowcroft Cemetery.

A blasphemous farmer living in the nearby wild uplands decided that tombstones from the burial ground would be more useful in his cellars and on his farm than 'hiding the clay of such as these'. So one night he carted all the tombstones away. The spirits of the tombs haunted him and his household forever afterwards. There were many eerie happenings at the farm. Milk went sour without cause and cattle and horses died. Pansheons – earthenware bowls used to separate cream from milk – seemed to dance on the gravestones on which they had been placed. Whenever there was a storm, spirits howled. The farmer's son was killed when a spirit leaped out onto his horse from the burial ground one night. Soon afterwards the farmer's wife was taken ill and died.

At last the farmer, 'feared, maddened and distracted', harnessed all his horses in the dead of night and took the slabs back more quickly than he fetched them. But he never saw happiness again.

A similar story is related in connection with Underbank Unitarian Chapel on Stopes Rd.

Although its galleries and box pews were removed in 1867, Underbank is still one of the finest examples of an eighteenth century chapel. An earlier building was erected nearby in 1652 as a chapel of ease in this isolated corner of Ecclesfield Parish and the congregation, numbering 350 in 1715, always inclined towards the dissenting cause. The present building was

erected in 1742-3 in local squared stone, when the old building, built by the Presbyterian Richard Spoone, during the Protectorate, became so worm-eaten in the pews and floor that the congregation preferred to use the galleries.

When the Act of Uniformity was passed in 1662, Underbank, with four or five others in the diocese of York, was not included among the churches of the Establishment, probably because it was so remote and not considered worth looking after.

Consequently, owing to the preaching of a Unitarian minister, Mr Moore, whom the congregation invited there, the church became Unitarian and a new church was built in 1828 for those who preferred the Anglican way.

It is not surprising in such a heated religious atmosphere that Anglicans should feel no reverence for Dissenters' graves. The story goes that the folk who lived at Brook Side Farm after the family of Shaw, used the Shaw gravestones for stone tables in their cellar and placed pans of milk on them. They were punished, however, as the ghosts of the Shaws came out every night and made such a rattling and squealing that the desecrators were only too eager to take the stones back, though not without difficulty as their horses refused to pull the cart to Underbank churchyard.

Clearly there has been a mix up as the tale has spread from mouth to mouth, for the Shaw gravestones are now to be found in the windswept Quaker burial ground, officially Bowcroft Cemetery. The inscription for George Shaw, late of Brook Side, who died on 5th May 1708 says that 'He suffered much for bearing his testimony against the payment of tithes'. Clearly he was a Quaker, not a Unitarian, who would have been allowed burial at Underbank. The other stones are for his wife, his brother William of Hill Farm, and William's wife and mother-in-law.

Around 1975, a certain man cut stakes from the Quaker burial ground to prop up his beans. All the beans promptly withered and died.

Hathersage Churchyard

Little John's Grave

··

ACCORDING TO one version of the old legend, Little John was a nailmaker's apprentice who was a follower of Simon de Montfort. When the rebels were defeated by the Earl of Leicester in 1265, he and many others of the rebel army took to the forests. He is said to have met Robin Hood at Clifton upon Calder.

After he buried Robin at Kirklees, he returned to his family home at Hathersage to end his days. The one-roomed cottage, according to legend still owned by the Little family into the nineteenth century, stood within a hundred yards of the grave. Unfortunately, it was pulled down in 1882 and the stones used to build a garden wall.

In 1933 a stranger interested in the legend and in anatomy – a certain Captain James Shuttleworth – bribed the sexton of Hathersage, Philip Heaton, to open the grave, where he found human bones of a great size. He tipped the sexton handsomely and went off with the bones. Ill-luck followed both of them. The sexton became twisted with rheumatism and soon he was going blind. At night he was haunted by nameless fears. It was with relief that he saw the stranger return with the bones a year later. The stranger seemed very eager to part with them and the sexton was glad to re-bury them. Immediately their troubles ceased.

John's six-foot longbow, arrows and suit of chainmail used to be kept in Hathersage Church, later placed in Cannon Hall, near Barnsley, Their present whereabouts are unknown.

St. Michael's Parish Church

The Old Vicarage, Hathersage
....

WHEN THE REVEREND John Le Cornu from Jersey became vicar in 1796 he decided that the vicarage was too small for his needs and extended it. Then the Reverend Henry Nussey (whose proposal Charlotte Brontë refused) extended the house again for his wealthy bride, Ellen, whom he married in 1845. It was extended again under the Reverend J.H. Brooksbank, who was vicar from 1910.

The seven-bedroomed house was too big and inconvenient for modern, servantless clergy, who found it too costly to run. A new vicarage was built behind it on the Croft and the old house was sold by auction in October 1984. It is now run as a B & B, yet retains its seventeenth-century charm.

An attraction is undoubtedly the legend of the White Lady. She was seen by the Reverend Brooksbank. Nowadays she is said to open a certain door every year on the night of 28th February.

Loxley Motors

(St. Mark's Methodist Chapel), 192 Loxley Road
....

ST. MARK'S METHODIST CHAPEL was built in 1834. It was so small that the Sunday School Anniversary sermons were held in Woodland View Primitive Methodist Chapel for several years. Then in 1870 the chapel was enlarged to seat 150 people. Many members could not read or write so preachers recited hymns for the congregation to memorise.

During the Sheffield Flood of 1864 when the Dale Dyke Dam burst, people sought refuge in the church and when the waters subsided, bodies were found inside.

As the population increased, in 1898 it was decided to build a new chapel, and the present site on Dykes Lane was acquired. The new chapel, built for £4,000 and seating 430, opened on 29th December 1904. The old one was used for Sunday School until after the war, when a wooden building was erected behind the new chapel.

The old chapel was sold in 1922 to the Salvation Army, who used it as their mission hall until they in turn sold it. In 1948 Harry Hodgson and Sons Ltd, motor engineers, opened their business there. In 1959 it became Loxley Motors and has retained that name under various owners.

In September 1984, Steven Shaw and Alan Widdowson were there. They described how a former owner in the 1970s was painting a car, when he saw the apparition of a woman. He fled, never to return, and sold the business. One previous owner, Graham Dennell who often worked there late at night and heard noises he could not explain. The back door was on a catch, but it sometimes opened and shut by itself, making him 'jump a mile'.

A man was working beneath the floor when he heard footsteps directly above him. He went up to look, but found the place empty. Others have heard a clanging sound, as if from a busy workshop, even when no-one else was there.

Mr Shaw and Mr Widdowson said that it got unnaturally cold at nights, even in the summer, and polythene on the window flapped even when there was no wind. They frequently saw what could be a mouse out of the corner of a eye, but when they looked around there was nothing. There were no other signs of mice. Was it a phantom mouse or something more sinister?

A man who stayed behind to paint some car wheels at a bench, heard what he thought was someone behind him. Looking round, he saw no-one. He hurriedly locked up and left, and then to his dismay realised that he had left his own keys behind. Shaking he forced himself to go back for them, but only felt safe when he was out of the building again.

Attercliffe Unitarian Chapel

(Jamiyat Mosque), 19 Shirland Lane
....

W HEN TWO YOUNG MEN of the McKean family of Oldbury, Birmingham, settled in Attercliffe they found that the Unitarian Upper Chapel in the city centre was too far to visit regularly, so they began meetings in their own houses, forming the Attercliffe Unitarian School and Church. As membership increased, they hired rooms at Attercliffe Vestry Hall and then bought land in Shirland Lane for their own chapel, which opened in 1907.

At first, music was provided by a harmonium from Upper Chapel. Then each family in the congregation gave £1 to buy a piano. The chapel piano was a remarkable instrument. People living nearby regularly heard it playing by itself when the chapel was locked up for the night.

After the Second World War, the population of Attercliffe, already growing less, dwindled even more as the area was increasingly devoted to industry and houses were pulled down. The last regular minister left in 1937 and lay preachers and district ministers served at the chapel until it finally closed. By 1968 it had become the Jamiyat Mosque. The building was destroyed by fire in 1981, and after a gale on Tuesday 14th January 1986 made the building unsafe, it had to be demolished.

Beauchief Abbey

Off Abbey Lane
....

T HE ABBEY WAS FOUNDED in 1175 by Robert FitzRanulph in expiation for his part in the murder of Thomas à Becket in 1170. Its parent abbey was Prémontré in France and the monks, from the colour of their habits, were called the White Canons. After the Dissolution of the monasteries, its land was given to the local gentry and the abbey itself fell into decay. Only part of it now remains as the Parish Church of St Thomas à Becket.

Bradfield Parish Church

....

T HE PARISH CHURCH of St. Nicholas, High Bradfield, was constructed in the fifteenth century, re-using some of the stone from an earlier church on the same site.

The church was built as close as possible to the huge earthwork known as Bailey Hill, which was probably a religious site and important meeting place in pre-Christian times. No excavations have been undertaken but a local legend says that a

great treasure is buried there. An underground passage is said to run from Bailey Hill through the churchyard to Castle Hill, the remains of an ancient fort.

A story is told of how the site of the church was to have been in Low Bradfield, near the Cross Inn, where the eighth century Anglo-Saxon stone cross (now in St. Nicholas') was dug up in 1870. However, each night the building materials were moved by unseen hands to Bailey Hill.

The church stands 860 feet above sea-level and is mostly built in the Perpendicular style (1399-1547). Originally it was a chapel of ease with visiting priests walking to Bradfield to take the services. In 1868 the church became independent of Ecclesfield and the building was restored in 1870. After 1858 burials were forbidden inside any church, so extra land was bought for £160 to increase the churchyard. The Watch House was built in 1745 to guard newly buried corpses from body-snatchers, who sold them to medical schools. The round house with its many windows is the last surviving watchhouse in Yorkshire.

Two curious stories are told in connection with the churchyard. In the 1980s a Sheffield man was exploring the churchyard when he tripped up and fell across a grave. To his horror he saw his own name on the headstone. He never did find out if his namesake, who had died many years previously, was an ancestor. However, the incident proved not to be an ill-omen, as he lived another ten years to tell the tale.

In the 1990s a woman in her early thirties died suddenly of a brain haemorrhage. After the funeral at Bradfield Church, the family took photographs of the flower-covered grave to send to her brother, who lived in Canada. No photographs had been taken of her in her coffin, so there was no question of one photograph being taken over another. The friend saw the developed prints. An image of her exactly as she looked in her coffin appeared among the flowers.

The Old Rectory
Church Lane, Aston
....

NOW CALLED HIGH TREES, the old Georgian Rectory stands next to All Saints' Church. A former rector, Reverend William Mason, a talented writer and musician, was a friend of Thomas Gray, the poet (1716-1771), whose *Elegy written in a Country Churchyard* was mostly written here. Mason suggested that the elegy be shortened. Some of the omitted lines were then written over the doorway of the summmer house, which unfortunately has since been demolished. However busts of the two friends, which also once adorned it, can now be found inside the church next door.

Mason himself was one-time chaplain to King George III and a friend of many literary giants of the age, including Horace Walpole, most of whom visited him at the rectory. He was passed over as Poet Laureate because of his outspoken opinions. The house is haunted by the ghost of a former rector, who caught his wife in the arms of the butler, and murdered her. There is an indelible bloodstain on the floor of the bedroom, where the murder took place.

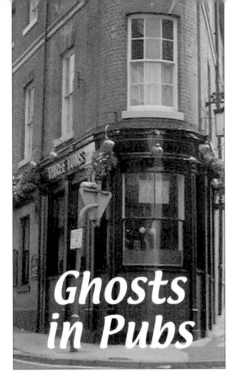

Ghosts in Pubs

Public houses are particularly favourable haunts for ghosts, not necessarily for the reasons put forward by cynics, but because of the age of many of the buildings.

The Ship Inn

312 Shalesmoor
....

THIS INN, in the oldest part of Sheffield, is over 200 years old. Beneath it is a warren of cellars and tunnels, many of which are now bricked up. One of the tunnels is known to have led to the Old Wharf on the Don, near the Ball Bridge, from which point smuggled liquor was brought up to the inn.

On the night of Friday 11th March 1864, the greatest peacetime tragedy England had known struck Sheffield, which then had a population of 150,000. The Dale Dyke Dam at Lower Bradfield, which held 700 million gallons of water in an area of seventy-eight acres, burst its banks. The water swept down upon Owlerton, 450 feet below it and over six miles away, and continued on to flood the city centre. At least 270 people were drowned and 798 houses were completely destroyed, 4,357 being damaged.

Some bodies were never recovered, among them those of two seamen who were in their boat heading up the tunnel towards the *Ship Inn*. When the tunnel became flooded, their boat was swamped and they were drowned.

One of the seamen, an old man of about sixty-five years, wearing a white scarf and a navy-blue jacket, and smoking a pipe, now haunts the inn.

Curiously enough, the landlady, Mrs Kathleen Stewart, and her husband did not meet him face to face in their twenty-four years at the inn, but other people have.

On one occasion several customers shouted to her that the seaman was standing behind her, but when she turned round he was already gone. One New Year's Eve they were having a party in the back room, when the barman, a hefty lad, went to use the phone in the bar. He came running back yelling that there was a white-haired man sitting out there. On another occasion a lad went down to the cellars. As he was coming back up, he found his way barred by the old smuggler. Panic-stricken, he had to run straight through him to get up.

The electrician who worked in the newly-opened part of the cellars when the Stewarts first moved in, kept finding the door into that cellar closed behind him. Only later did he realise that the ghost was responsible. The ghost has a habit of removing articles and then returning them weeks later. Mr Stewart's Italian silk shirt vanished from the wardrobe, only to reappear there months later. Mrs Stewart's sovereign on a chain and a matching bracelet vanished. They hunted everywhere for it, but concluded that it had been stolen. They decided to tell the police, but before they could do so, it was discovered lying on a dusty mantelpiece, where it certainly had not been before.

An old man uncannily resembling the ghost, according to customers, used to sit in the bar occasionally. No-one knew who he was and he rarely spoke to anyone. A university student painted a portrait of him smoking his pipe, with a very peaceful expression upon his face. At first the portrait was hung in the bar, then relegated to the cellar in the hope that the ghost would be induced to remain in the cellar too. When the author asked to see it, Mrs Stewart hunted for some time in the cellar and was unable to find it. Subsequent, more thorough searches of the entire pub, have been in vain. Has the old smuggler appropriated it because he was shy of seeing it published?

Ten days before the sinking of *HMS Sheffield* near the Falkland Islands on May 4th 1982, a steel-framed picture of the ship fell down from the wall of the pub. At the time everyone regarded it as an ill omen.

In 1986, a man in a striped shirt was seen by five customers seated in a corner with a pint in his hand, but the landlord had not seen him or served him.

In May 1987 when the Stewarts retired, their daughter Jeanette, who had lived at the pub all her life, took over the license with her husband, Steve Rodgers. It was then owned by Stones' Brewery. In 1991 they sold it to Tomlinsons.

Jeanette had never actually seen anything, but on one occasion when she went down into the cellar, she tried to open the door and it was shut against her leg by an unseen hand.

Nicky, a barmaid, was in the ladies' toilets when an old man, not the sailor, walked in through one wall and out by another wall. Two or three women have had the experience of going to open a cubicle door there and having it shut in their faces, when no-one else was there.

Not so long ago, a workman came out of the cellar, shaking like a leaf. His tool box had turned upside down by itself.

Acorn Inn

288-292 Shalesmoor
....

IN THE WINTER OF 1960-61 the old Acorn Inn, a pub since 1825, was derelict, apart from the cellar which was rented for three nights a week by Club 60, a group of jazz fans.

The cellar, which is large and divided by archways, had a sinister reputation. It was said to be haunted by the spirit of a man who had been murdered and buried there forty years before. The wife of one of the club members was sweeping the floor when something brushed past her accompanied by a rush of wind. Once after the cellar was unlocked, a jar of pennies used for decoration were found scattered behind the coffee bar.

On 7th February 1961, Cedric Morris of Holmesfield accepted his friends' dare to sleep there alone, despite a warning from Mr William Osgathorpe, a student of psychical research, that he could very well scare himself to death. Taking a guitar, sleeping bag, sandwiches and coffee, he settled down for the night on the spot where the murdered man had been buried. He posed for a *Star* photographer, who found that, though he tried six times to take a picture, the flash would not work until Cedric moved his sleeping bag from that particular spot.

He was locked in at eleven o'clock and was to stay there until seven in the morning. As a precaution, he had a key. He tried to keep calm by composing a tune on his guitar, 'If you were the only ghoul in the world', but the ghost was sadly lacking in musical appreciation. At six-thirty, Cedric rushed out, terrified, unable to stand it any longer.

He reported that he had not seen anything but, 'Every so often I felt a rushing of wind around me and a strange feeling that I wasn't alone. All the night there was a weird creaking that I've never heard before down there.'

The old inn was taken over by the Albert Jackson heating and bathroom centre, which closed down in 2000. The staff had heard that it was the ghost of a man who had hanged himself. Or was he murdered by hanging? Either way would account for the creaking Cedric heard.

In the bathroom showroom upstairs there is a presence, not cold or frightening, just something which makes you feel that you are not alone. Yet you look around and see no-one there. The cellar is especially eerie at dusk and early in the morning, and staff did not like to be alone there then. Used for storage, its walls are still painted a garish yellow and purple and one wall is still decorated with bottles from the nearby *Ship Inn*, a relic of Club 60.

Scruffy Murphy's

Once the Mail Coach Inn,
149 West Street

·····································

THE *MAIL COACH*, legend tells, used to be a coaching inn. Dick Turpin apparently haunts half the pubs in Sheffield, but this is not one of them. The ghost here wears a cap and loose mac. Moreover, it became an inn long after Turpin was hung at York in 1739 and after the mail coaches ceased to run to London in the early 1840s.

The connection with Turpin is the result of two men, who were divers, coming from Blackpool in 1979 to look for a well where Dick Turpin was supposed to have dumped his loot, when he was being closely pursued by Bow Street Runners. The *Mail Coach* had a well, now covered up, in the cellar, so they thought that must be the right pub.

In fact, there are traces of old wells all over the city, many connected with inns long since closed down.

The history of the *Mail Coach* is confusing. There was a *Mail Coach Inn* at No.33 West Street mentioned in the 1833 directory, though not in 1828 or 1837. In 1839 the *Mail Coach Inn* with Esther Eyre as proprietress was at No.131 West Street. By 1841 its name was changed to the *Royal Mail*.

From 1868 to 1872 the *Mail Coach* at No.131 had been taken over by William Eyre, but he had moved to No.151 in 1876. In the 1872 directory William Eyre was described as also being a cooper and packing-case maker at Gas Office yard, Bow Street. In 1879, Francis Oldfield, victualler, was at No.151. In 1881, Thos. Hy. Eyre was at the *Mail Coach Inn*, but in 1889 Mrs Ruth Hewitt was a victualler at No.149.

From then on, the history of Tetley's

Mail Coach is fairly straight-forward. The eastern half of the present bar has always been part of the pub, but the other half at various times has been a photocopying shop and a hairdressers.

The landlord, Mr Walter Scott, there since 1979, experienced strange happenings from 1981. On separate occasions he and a customer saw a slim man in a cap and a loose mac walk from the locked entrance door across the bar floor to the men's toilets, which were converted from the old stables. The man seemed solid enough but they did not see his face.

The customer was puzzled enough to check where he had gone to, but the door to the toilets was also locked and there was no-one in the kitchen.

On one occasion in 1984, about six-thirty in the evening, another customer, who was standing at the side of the bar, was pushed out of the way by the ghost, clear across to the record player. There was no-one else near him at the time.

Mr Scott, at the bar after hours, saw the man out of the corner of his eye seated in the corner of the lounge. A woman customer also saw him seated there. Perhaps it used to be his favourite seat when he was alive. It is unfortunate that no-one has seen his face clearly so that he could perhaps be identified.

In recent years at least, staff have seen nothing. It is at present an Irish theme pub, renamed *Scruffy Murphy's* in 1994.

Manor Castle Inn

239 Manor Lane

....

BUILT AMID the ruins of Manor Castle, which dates from early in the reign of Henry VIII, little remains of the original building on the site, a small passageway upstairs, two wide, low doors and one room, while the downstairs room has been incorporated into one large taproom. The old doorway also remains to the cellar.

It opened as a beerhouse, run by Joseph Walker, in 1919. He was succeeded by his widow, Mrs Annie E. Walker until 1936. When Henry Osborne took over in 1937 it was elevated to the status of an inn.

In November 1983, a new landlord, Jack Wright, his wife and three-year-old daughter Francine moved in. Three weeks later they moved out, driven by events which had begun two days after their arrival, when Mr Wright saw a white, human-shaped figure in the bedroom.

Their dog also saw it and started barking, whereupon the ghost disappeared into the wardrobe. Francine saw the ghost several times and described it as wearing gaiters and a plumed hat.

Mrs Pat Wright also saw it. They always felt that they were never on their own.

However, Mrs Carol Barker, landlady from March 1985, saw nothing until 1986 when she and her son Lee were watching *Brookside* on television and the outline of an Elizabethan soldier appeared on the screen. Her mother-in-law saw the soldier upstairs. He has also been seen downstairs behind the bar. In 1986, her brother saw him in a field outside.

Since November 1991, the pub has been owned by Allied Breweries. One day a workman was sent to mend a sink downstairs. The mother-in-law saw a man upstairs and thought he was also from the brewery, so she made him a cup of tea too.

A heavy plastic curtain across the cellar moves of its own accord, although there are no draughts. Sometimes a heavy bunch of keys in the back door will start swinging violently.

Devonshire Arms

387 Herries Road, Firvale

·····································

WHEN THE *Devonshire Arms* at number 9-11, The Moor was bombed during the Second World War, Whitbreads put up a prefabricated hut on farmland at Firvale where the present car park is. Then, in 1962, they opened the newly-built *Devonshire Arms* behind it.

Mrs Wilson, landlady since 1969, had an open mind about the ghost at the pub, but acknowledged that queer things had happened at irregular intervals over the years. Beer barrels had been found turned off when they should have been on and vice versa (Sheffield ghosts seem to be fascinated by beer barrels); wine bottles had jumped out of their racks and cupboard doors have sprung open.

Fat Cat

23 Alma Street

···············

DOWN THE ROAD from Kelham Island Museum stands a three-storey Victorian monument to the spirit of the British soldier. Once named the *Alma Hotel*, after the British victory at Alma in the Crimea on 20th September 1854, it has since 2nd August 1981 become famous as the *Fat Cat*, Sheffield's first real ale free house, which, run by Dave Wickett, a Polytechnic lecturer and solicitor Bruce

Bentley, on its first anniversary received the CAMRA (Campaign for Real Ale) Pub of the Year award. Nowadays, as well as selling a variety of interesting beers, they brew their own beers next to the pub at the Kelham Island Brewery.

Since being built in the late 1850s, until some time before the Second World War, the pub was also a boarding house for itinerant steel workers, with rooms upstairs for at least ten guests. On 29th April 1912 it was sold to William Stones Ltd. of the nearby Cannon Brewery, Rutland Road, by Thomas Richardson, a retired bank manager, Fred Bannister Wigfull, a brewer, Henry Reed, a solicitor, and Ibbotson Bros. & Co. Ltd. of the Globe Steel Works.

When Stones re-sold it in 1981 it had a falling clientele. The landlord between 1975 and 1981 was Frank Nicholson. He knew that the undistinguished outer appearance of the pub masked strange goings-on. Once, when he was in the kitchen alone late at night, a vegetable rack suddenly shot across the floor. On another occasion something, tried to push him downstairs.

The beer in the cellar would be found turned on, when it should be off, and vice-versa. Doors banged and footsteps were heard when there was no-one there. Joan, his wife, irritated, would call out 'Shut up, Mary!' and all would be quiet for a while.

The ghost is known as Workhouse Mary, from her workhouse uniform. An old woman, she was seen in 1982 by a worker at the firm across the road, Woodhead Components. He rushed into the *Fat Cat*, white as a sheet, seeking something liquid to soothe his nerves.

Mary was an inmate of the Sheffield Union Workhouse, which stood opposite the *Alma Hotel*. The building was converted from a cotton mill in 1829, built in 1811 on the site of earlier mills burned down in 1792 and 1810. (Hence Cotton Mill Row).

By 1856, the Poor Law Board, realising that it was utterly inadequate, required the Guardians to purchase land for a new workhouse at Firvale. Meanwhile, the Kelham Street building was enlarged in 1859 to accommodate 1,200 inmates instead of 900. One visitor had found thirteen women in one room sharing eight beds.

There was no special provision for the sick, except during 1832 when the top floor of the workhouse was used as an isolation unit for victims of the great cholera epidemic. Lunatics were chained up, but slept and ate with the other inmates.

Apart from her first name, nothing is known about Mary. Did she die in the workhouse in strikened circumstances?

brigade for training exercises.

It is not very old as pubs go, but has already acquired the ultimate attraction – a resident ghost, said to be that of a barmaid who hanged herself from the attic rafters when she discovered that she was pregnant.

In an account in the *South Yorkshire Times* in January 1975, landlord Fred Jow and his wife Lily said that although they had moved in only six months before, they had already heard strange bangings and clumpings in the night and felt extreme cold in various parts of the building. Cleaners who once worked in the pub have seen a young girl in a grey dress wandering in the long passages upstairs. She is very thin, with a pale drawn look.

One of the attic rooms was kept locked and Mrs Jow said she had no intention of opening it. There was definitely some kind of presence in the bathroom on the top floor. Their daughter, who was twenty-five years old and a very down-to-earth person, went up there but did not stop to investigate. Shelves kept falling down for no reason. One relief manager was so frightened that he took a pick-axe handle to bed with him. Another relief manager refused to stay overnight when he discovered a Zodiac sign and a claw-hand on one of the upstairs walls.

The ghost has done no-one any harm but has certainly frightened several people. However, Mr Fawthrop, landlord at the *Ball Inn* from October 1993 has seen nothing.

Ball Inn
287 Darnall Road
················

THE *Ball Inn*, now owned by Courage Brewery, was built in 1910 and is one of the tallest buildings in Darnall, being used at one time by the local fire

Wellington Inn
222 Main Road, Darnall
·····························

THE WHITE LADY at the *Wellington Inn* dates from the times when it was a manor house. She is a little old lady, whose husband hid his money before he died. She is still searching for it.

There is apparently a second ghost. In January 1975 in the *South Yorkshire Times,* the landlady of the *Wellington Inn,* Mrs Margaret Roebuck, who had recently moved in with her husband and sister, described how she was surprised to see the figure of a man pass by the door of one of the upstairs rooms. She was told by one of the customers that it was probably 'Big Jim' Elliott, who had kept the pub fifteen years previously and had haunted it for some time.

However, Mrs Lazenby, who moved in during 1979, saw nothing. Margaret Hackett, at the inn since 1989 also saw nothing.

Florist Inn

185 Walkley Road

THE *FLORIST INN* is about three hundred years old. High on a hill, it was conveniently placed at a point where horses pulling coaches had to stop to rest before going the rest of the way up. Nowadays exhausted pedestrians who have struggled up from Langsett Road are welcomed there.

The landlord in 1982, Bill Kidd, described the antics of his unofficial guest. On one occasion he had unplugged all the coolers in order to clean out the pipes. An hour later he heard them humming and realised that someone (or something) had put the plug back in and switched them on again. The emergency lights switched themselves on and off. Lady customers complained that the toilet doors opened by themselves. Once someone tapped Mr Kidd on the shoulder, but when he turned round there was no-one there. Once he heard someone calling him from upstairs. On investigating, he found no-one. Another time he was playing darts in the back room, when he heard footsteps in the bar. Again no-one.

Their labrador dog refused to come downstairs to the ground floor unaccompanied during the daytime. At night, he would not come down at all, but just stood at the head of the stairs barking. Did he see what his master and mistress could not?

The pub changed hands three times over eight years. It was owned by John Smith's then by Entrepreneur Estates and Elders have now taken over. Keith Wainwright, landlord from August 1983 saw nothing unusual.

The Red Lion

145 Duke Street

SITUATED BEHIND Park Hill Flats is an unexpected piece of Sheffield history. The *Red Lion* pub is at least two hundred years old and has happily retained its traditional atmosphere.

In 1707, the Duke of Norfolk's estate agent had the woodlands around the later Duke Street cleared for farmland. The first building on the site of the pub was probably a farmhouse.

On March 6th 1781, Jonathan Gould leased a messuage (a house with outbuildings) from the Norfolk estate for £1-11s-6d per annum. We cannot be sure if it was then a pub as the map shows a different outline of the building than today's.

However, a 1797 map shows a building with the present outline, together with a brewhouse.

It is not certain from where the name of the pub came. The coat of arms of the Dukes of Norfolk included a red lion and that of the Earls of Shrewsbury had a red background with gold lions. Furthermore at about the time when the pub was opened an Irish noble, Talbot was a naval commander. His coat of arms had a red lion on a silver background. Pubs were often named after contemporary heroes.

In 1758 Thomas Rawson and Sons set up as brewers on Pond Street. At that time few brewers owned pubs and the practice of having tied houses did not become general practice until the 1870s. Joshua Tetley did not own any pubs until 1890. However, by 1800 Rawsons were taking over pubs and making them into tied houses, selling only their own beer. By 1813, Rawsons leased three pubs on Duke Street alone – the *Red Lion*, the *Crown* (1825-1902) and the *Robin Hood* (1825-1950). Rawsons (who once employed Samuel Plimsoll as a clerk for £1 a week) leased the *Red Lion* some time between 1798 and 1813 and bought it in 1891 for £1,300.

Rawsons' 1815 survey of all their pubs show that the *Red Lion* had a brewhouse where the present kitchen is and a well in the far corner of the yard. A new roof was put on in the second half of the nineteenth century.

The first publican known by name was John Belk, 1825-1835. There was a stone quarry nearby and the workers and carters were good customers as were the residents of the atrocious slums round about. The *Red Lion*'s yard opened onto Weigh Lane, which led to the quarry. In the 1870s there were 15 pubs on Duke Street alone.

There were many illegal gambling rackets and on one occasion in 1916 troops with fixed bayonets could be seen running down Duke Street. Between the two world wars gang warfare was a fact of life in the district, but the strong character of the *Red Lion*'s licensee, John Pownall (1914-36) kept the pub out of it. There were no after-hours drinking convictions there.

Rawsons were taken over by Duncan Gilmour and Company in 1946. In 1954 Gilmours merged with Tetleys. Then in 1992, as a result of the Monopolies and Mergers Commission, larger breweries had to sell some of their pubs and the *Red Lion* was sold to Burtonwoods.

It retains its quiet, traditional atmosphere with a pool and darts teams and fishing and social clubs. In July 1993 the licensee, a former silverware industry man Paul Hodson and his wife Anne told stories of its ghost, who was held responsible for the gaming machines and cooler being found switched off when they should have been on. Staff under the licensee in 1997, Kathleen Silvester, reckoned that if you believe in ghosts, you'll see them; if you don't believe in them, you won't.

The Station Hotel
732 Attercliffe Road
....

B UILT IN 1833, it was originally three two-roomed cottages. The ghost is said to be someone who was knifed to death in one of the cottages.

The landlord in 1982, George Huttley, described how glasses of beer were tipped up for no apparent reason and footsteps were heard on the first floor when no-one was there.

Late one evening the pubful of customers heard footsteps come down the stairs and saw the door open, but no-one came through it.

Nothing was seen by the landlady, Mrs Hattersley, who moved in in March 1994.

The Big Tree

842 Chesterfield Road, Woodseats

....

O FFICIALLY it was called *The Mason's Arms*, but by popular request of its customers, the name was finally changed to what the local people had always called it anyway. Which is as it should be. After all, the tree has always been more famous than the pub itself.

According to *Kelly's Directory,* at *The Mason's Arms* in 1854 the landlady was Anna Seddon and in 1860 the landlord was William Marshall. In 1862, however, the name was changed to *The Mason's Arms and Sycamore Tree* under the new landlord, John Cadman.

Records show that a *Mason's Arms* has been on the same site for over a hundred and sixty years. In the Derbyshire Directory for 1835 we find at Woodseats, then a small village outside Sheffield, the *Freemason's Arms* with Joseph Seddon as victualler. The present building was constructed in 1901. A relic of the old inn – a portion of the mosaic floor with the name *Mason's Arms* on it – was retained.

The original big tree in front of the inn was a huge beech. John Wesley had preached under it on a Sunday evening and Francis Chantrey, who had been orphaned at the age of twelve and in 1797 apprenticed to a wood-carver and frame-maker in Sheffield, carved effigies of local folk from old cart shafts under the tree. In the early 1900s, when Sanger's Circus visited Sheffield, some elephants were tethered to the tree. One of them broke off a main branch. Afterwards the tree withered and died. Mr Baldwin Young quickly provided a replacement from his orchard at Gleadless.

In 1995, this tree, having succumbed to Dutch Elm disease, was cut down, to be replaced by a 20-foot high sapling.

The landlord in 1982 was not convinced that there was a ghost. In charge since 1977 he had heard only a mysterious clicking noise occasionally in one of the bedrooms, which he put down to the old structure of the building. The young son of a former landlord, however, is reported to have been bothered by a poltergeist.

The *Big Tree* was turned by Whitbreads into an American-style Brewburger restaurant. re-opening on October 27th 1982 with Peter Yates and his fiancée, Jill Saxby as joint managers. During their three months there they learned that the relief manageress before them had seen the ghost of a man, but they themselves experienced nothing.

Joanna, who worked there after May 1992 described how glasses were found smashed in the empty glass washroom and things were always falling off the kitchen shelves by themselves. Her mother-in-law, who is psychic, sensed an unseen presence.

The Woodseats

743 Chesterfield Road, 8

....

O RIGINALLY CALLED *The Woodseats Hotel*, and more recently known as the *Floozie and Firkin*, this pub was built on the site of two cottages, when the street level was lower than today. Happily, in March 2000 the pub reverted to its old name, *The Woodseats.*

The public house was mentioned in the 1879 *Kelly's Directory,* when William Jackson was landlord. It was then counted as being in the village of Norton. By 1896 under Mrs Ellen Barker it was in Norton Woodseats. In 1898 it was listed as being at 305 Chesterfield Road, in 1902 at No.457. In 1910, when George William Woodhead was landlord, the houses on Chesterfield Road having again been renumbered, it was at last No.743.

Suitably refurbished, during the 1990s it was renamed the *Floozie and Firkin*, but the new licensee reported nothing unusual, even though the previous occupants, Mark and Fay Middlebrook and their teenage son, Dean, were eventually driven out by the ghostly goings-on.

On the Monday after Mark and Fay moved in, Mark was showing the barmaid how to work the pumps, when something pushed the girl's head against the pump. Fay was nowhere near. In the summer of 1994 Fay was on her own, when she stooped to reach a glass. Suddenly icy fingers curled round the back of her head. Then they rammed her forehead into a pump.

The gas taps in the cellar were turned off mysteriously on several occasions. Then the cider pump suddenly began dispensing beer. Mark checked that the barrels were properly connected. 'When I pulled the cider pump again, beer still came out. As I watched the stream, it slowly turned into cider. Impossible!'

Glasses exploded without warning at any time of the day, notably on Sunday 11th September 1995. Barmaid Lorraine Richardson had just opened up in the evening. 'I'd picked up a glass when it expanded in my hand like a balloon. I could feel the pressure force my fingers apart. Then the glass exploded.'

The following Wednesday, Mark was ill in bed. On Thursday he came downstairs and asked where were the children, who had been laughing. There were no children in the pub or in the street. The sound of laughing children was heard on other occasions by other people in the pool area. Thirty years previously a boy had been burned to death next door. Was there any connection?

On another occasion, while next door's roof was being replaced, Dean saw a man seated at the other side of the pub, only to vanish in the split second when his attention was distracted.

It was probably the same man seen by customer Andrew Parking at Christmas 1993. He was drinking at the bar, when he glanced behind him and saw an old man seated at a table in the far corner. He wore a flat cap and trenchcoat and was staring at the wall. Andrew asked Fay: 'Does he want serving?' 'Who?' she asked. 'You're the only customer.' Andrew turned and saw that the old man had vanished! That was when he realised he'd seen a ghost. He rushed out, leaving his beer unfinished.

One Thursday night in November 1993 Fay had made some stew and dumplings. After Dean had eaten, he left the pan on a coffee table. In the morning the stew was found thrown over the settee, but the pan was still on the table. An ash-tray was tipped up, but replaced on the table, as was a cup.

Fay was in the toilet, when a coat detached itself from a hook and floated the length of the passageway to land on the floor. On another occasion in the Ladies she watched as the poltergeist unravelled the toilet roll and tore it up all over the floor. Two women customers told how they had seen the ghost of an old woman in the Ladies some years previously.

On the Saturday night after the incident of the coat Mark and a friend were playing pool downstairs, while Fay lay in bed. There came a loud knocking on the bedroom door but no-one was there.

A few days before Christmas 1994 their dogs in the upstairs flat began howling and continued all day, fur on end and teeth bared. They were seeing something the Middlebrooks could not see.

Waggon and Horses

Abbeydale Road, Millhouses
....

NEAR ONE OF the entrances to Millhouses Park, the *Waggon and Horses* used to be an old coaching inn. The first owner is recorded as being Richard Bagshawe – possibly one of the Bagshawes of Norton – in 1725.

On the night of October 11th 1786 a charcoal burner named George Yardley, who was related to the family who then owned the inn, drank too much beer for lunch there and when he went back to his work in nearby Ecclesall Woods, accidently set his cabin on fire and burned to death. He was buried in the woods, where his grave is still to be seen, by four friends,

Will Brooke, a salesman, David Glossop, a gamekeeper, Thos. Smith, a besom-maker and Sampson Brookeshaw, of the *Rising Sun Inn*. He is said to haunt the woods because he was buried on unconsecrated ground.

It may not be he who haunts the *Waggon and Horses*, although someone called Three-pint Jack – so called because he drank from a three-pint mug – does so. A lady customer recalled hearing one landlord, who moved out because he could stand the strain no longer, complain about 'that ruddy ghost playing his violin upstairs'. Perhaps the ghost's musical talents were limited! Legend has it that the highwayman, Dick Turpin and his horse, Black Bess, used to stay there, her hoofbeats are still to be heard in the yard.

Geoffrey Evans, who moved in as landlord during 1975, did not actually see anything, but often got the impression that there was someone in the place with him, even when he knew he was alone. His dog used to suddenly jump up and bark furiously at the wall as if he had seen something, and he would never go into the cellar. An assistant barman once spent the night there and heard footsteps in the corridor, but no-one was there.

A later landlord, who moved in at the beginning of December 1985, heard various odd noises – such as a grating sound at 4am – which he could not explain entirely

as the natural movements of an old house. The burglar alarm, which was sensitive to movement, went off twice within his first month at the pub. The dog developed a strange habit of licking at certain walls in the kitchen and the old part of the building until she was able to bite off a piece of plaster. Then she suddenly bolted up the corridor as if frightened by something.

In May 1993, the *Waggon and Horses* was bought by the Tom Cobleigh company, who converted it back to a pub from being a Harvester restaurant. It re-opened in November 1993 with Steve and Shirley Conroy in charge.

The staff call the ghost 'Flat Cap' after seeing pictures of George Yardley, but have not actually seen him. The bar flap slams by itself. The clock strikes thirteen – which could of course be due to faulty mechanism. The dog suddenly goes crazy, barking at a certain wall.

Carbrook Hall Hotel

537 Attercliffe Common
· ·

A BUILDING WAS recorded on the site of Carbrook Hall as long ago as 1176, when it was owned by the Blunt family. In the reign of Elizabeth I a Richard Fenton resided there. The Hall, which was built in 1462 stood a little further to the right of the present building and was pulled down between 1777 and 1819.

The present Hall was built by Stephen Bright who was born in Norton in 1583 and it continued in the possession of the Bright family or their connections by marriage, including the Earls Fitzwilliam until 1819.

Stephen's son, John Bright, was a Colonel in the Parliamentary army during the Civil War and led the attack upon Sheffield Castle. He became its governor when it was surrendered by the Royalists in 1644. From 1649 to 1660 he was governor of York and Hull and High Sheriff of the County of York 1654-55. He was made a baronet by Charles II and died in 1688.

In 1819 the Hall was sold by Admiral Frank Sotheran (1776-1861) to Thomas Booth and Company, who sold it to George Bradford, who owned almost all Attercliffe Common and much agricultural land towards Tinsley.

In 1855, the owners were the River Don Company and the tenants the Carbrook Land Society. From then on the Hall deteriorated into a 'common beer house'.

The most ancient part of the building dates from 1623 and the parlour, which is the most carefully preserved room with its oak panels, excellent moulded ceiling plaster work and the unusual carving on the oak fireplace, must have changed little from the days when the parliamentary army leaders held conferences there to discuss plans for attacking Sheffield Castle, which was later demolished on Cromwell's order.

Today John Bright, or at least a man in Puritan dress, is only one of several ghosts who haunt the *Carbrook Hall Hotel*. Members of the Society for Psychic Research have visited it. The landlady in 1982, Mrs Linda Butler, saw with them a roundhead in black cap and tall white collar. It was not the first time Mrs Butler had seen him since she moved in during 1978.

A customer, Bridget Beaumont, has seen him by the doorway near the cigarette machine at the end of the bar. She has also seen a little old lady, in early twentieth-century dress, near the same doorway, perhaps the same old lady seen by a previous landlord seated upstairs in a rocking chair. The landlady's sister in 1980 saw an old man in a flat cap pass the door of the parlour as she sat in the bar. In April 1982, a new ghost was seen.

A regular customer came out of the pool-room, very pale, and said that he had seen a monk-like figure in there, wearing a hood. However when he went back, it had gone. Mrs Butler said he was not the type to fool around or joke. When he came back, he was careful to sit on the other side of the pub.

Mrs Butler saw a glass come off a shelf and land on the floor, cheese move off the kitchen counter and a till drawer come out and land upside down on the floor. The door to the Jacobean room, the parlour, has opened and closed by itself. A certain table in the middle of the Jacobean room is not a good place to leave money. It apparently causes the money to disappear and then re-appear again.

On one occasion Bridget Beaumont was imprisoned in the first toilet by the ghost. She had her foot wedged in the doorway, but she felt her foot pushed aside, then the door closed. She struggled to open it, but had the impression that someone was holding it closed. Only when another woman entered the toilet, was it released.

Bridget has sensed other women in the bar. Several times she has left a cigarette burning in an ash-tray and has come back to find it moved around the edge of the ash-tray. On one occasion she turned quickly and saw the cigarette in mid-air floating back down to the ash-tray.

The bar is where the courtyard used to be and Bridget thinks that the man, probably John Bright himself, is just being curious about the way his house has changed. Sometimes the air in the bar becomes very cold and all the machines, including the television, are turned off by an unseen hand.

Once when this happened Bridget said, as she stood against the bar, 'I wouldn't mind him playing, if he'd show himself'.

Whereupon she was seized by unseen hands, propelled around the bar and, for the space of about twenty seconds, pinned against the cigarette machine. Then she had the sensation of being drawn through him. Other customers saw her unexplainedly propelled around the bar. The experience frightened her, although she was used to having strange things happen to her.

Bridget had been very close to her Uncle Billy, who had died in 1978. He had been a regular customer at the *Carbrook Hall Hotel*. On New Year's Eve 1980 she saw him standing in the corner by the juke box. She went over to him and, to the amazement of the other customers, who could of course see nothing unusual, she carried on a conversation with him. He asked her how she was and how was her mother and then said he would have to be going, but he would see her again. It was only after he had vanished that she remembered that he was dead, though she had felt very cold as she spoke to him.

A psychic researcher described how she saw the old Puritan on a visit in 1978, and how in the billiard room, when she asked if anyone was there, they should prove it, a billiard ball moved across the table and the heavy doors opened and closed. She sensed a definite atmosphere upstairs.

In 1990, Philip Skelton became the lessee. In 1993 he was going upstairs for some change, when he had the sensation that a big man was wanting to come down. He stood aside to let him pass. The ghost touched him on the arm as he passed, raising goose pimples. He disappeared near the corner at the bottom of the stairs. A man doing band practice in the Function Room also became aware of the big man, who was heavily dressed in thick dark green tweed.

When Mr Skelton stood in the bar, he often saw out of the corner of his eye someone go from the entrance towards the pool room, but the door never opened.

There have been some alterations in recent years. The Oak Room has been refurbished and the ceiling painted. The pool room's fireplace has been opened up. The cellar has been relined with breeze-blocks so it is now impossible to tell where the legendary tunnel is, which is said to run to what used to be Wragg's, the builders' merchants in Broughton Lane, now Kentucky Fried Chicken.

Saxon Hotel

Station Road, Kiveton Park

····························

THE *SAXON HOTEL* was built about 1959 but has built up a spooky reputation worthy of far older establishments, thanks largely to its resident ghost, Jasper the Whistler, aided by a Benedictine nun. Managers Linda and Brian Allen described how the ghosts have a habit of opening doors overnight which had been left closed, and turning on lights which had been turned off.

A professor from Sheffield University and the psychic investigator Simon Alexander confirmed the presence of mysterious entities.

Jasper is said to be a monk who was murdered. He whistles in the cellars as if trying to attract attention. Sometimes his presence in the cellars is so overpowering that anyone down there leaves as quickly as possible. He can often be heard padding down the cellar steps as if wearing slippers.

Just past the public house we find Chantry Place. The site of the chantry, the Chapel of the Holy Trinity at Kiveton was actually on Hard Lane Corner, where Hard Lane meets Station Road.

A charter was granted by Edward III (1327-1377) allowing John de Kyveton, parson of Radcliffe on Trent (a native of Kiveton and probably educated at Roche Abbey) to bestow on the Abbey of Roche 36 acres of ploughed land, three acres of meadow and 24 shillings' worth of rent yearly in Blithe and Torworth on condition that the abbot provided a secular chaplain to say mass for his ances-tors' souls every day and forever in the chapel of the Holy Trinity at Kiveton.

A charter of Henry IV, granted at Westminster on the 8th July 1401, repeated these conditions, but allowed the Abbot of Roche to make over the mentioned properties to the cantarist of.the chapel at Kiveton, who was thus to receive the income directly instead of through Roche Abbey. The chantry was entirely independant of Harthill Church.

A spring near the site of the chantry, known as Monk's Well or Monk's Spring, supplied the chantry with water.

The chantry was confiscated in 1538 by Henry VIII and completely destroyed, when Sir Richard Darvent or Darwent was cantarist.

Confiscated at the same time was a Benedictine nunnery at Wallingwells, which had owned land and tenements at Harthill since the time of King Stephen (1135-1154).

North Pole Inn

62 Sussex Street, Attercliffe

····························

ORIGINALLY A PRIVATE HOUSE called Riverside Cottage built in the nineteenth century, the *North Pole Inn* had a rear garden, which ran down to a mill pond beside the River Don.

Mick Short, who was licensee for two

years before it closed down in 1982, described the ghost, Tommy Jackson, who used to work as a night watchman for a nearby steel firm. He was distinctive-looking with his trilby hat and bulbous nose. Mick's wife saw him on several oocasions. Other people have also seen him since his death about 1900. He was blamed for turning off the beer taps when there were no living beings around.

The building is now occupied by True Print Business Forms. The managing director, Chris Hart said that he regularly smelled beer when he worked late, and a ghostly presence accompanied a staff member upstairs. Another staff member refused to work alone in the office.

Blue Stoops

High Street Dronfield Hill Top

....

THE *Blue Stoops Inn* has two 1596 date stones, one on the front of the building and the other over the fireplace in the right hand bar. These confirm that it was built in that year, although it was rebuilt in the eighteenth century. The left hand bar has a moulded stone chimney piece. For many years it was known as the *Blue Posts*. It could have originated in the medieval custom of painting the door posts of an inn a particular colour as a sign to travellers. The inn sign that existed at the end of the nineteenth century, however, showed two stoops or bollards at the entry of a yard to stop carts.

Mr Street, who was brought up at the Blue Stoops, recalled how it was when his grandfather was the landlord from 1882 to 1907. Beer was eight pints for a shilling and gin was 2^1/$_2$d. a glass. He recalled the six policemen ('rum uns') billeted there during the 1890 strike at the colliery near Gosforth Lane, and the women, smoking their long clay pipes, who sat in the bar. If they stayed too long at the pub, the menfolk, left minding the babies at home, would come to the pub and dump the babies in their laps.

The pub itself has changed little since Mr Street lived there, but it has acquired a ghost. A little girl used to walk around the ground floor. There is a rumour that she was illegitimate and was murdered, but how, when or by whom are lost in the mists of time. On 1st April 1980, there was a fire. The inn was then redecorated, but the little girl has never been seen since.

Tony Singleton became the landlord in 1989. Vaux Inns bought the pub from Wards in 1990. Occasionally a glass falls off a shelf for no apparent reason.

In August 1993 one of the regular customers died. A day or two before his funeral another regular was walking past on his way to work at 5.30am, when he saw that the lights were on in the bar and a man was standing there. Needless to say, the Singletons were not in the bar at that time!

Green Dragon Inn and Chantry Hotel

Church Street, Dronfield

....

THE INN and the hotel which share a party wall are probably both developments of the same medieval building.

The situation of the inn supports a tradition that it originally housed the chantry priests who prayed for the dead in the church opposite. There is a memorial in the chancel of the Church of St John the Baptist to two priests, the Gomfrey brothers. The building was also the headquarters of the Guild of the Blessed Virgin Mary, which was endowed in 1349. It probably became an inn when the chantrys and guilds were dissolved by Henry VIII. Nowadays its three storeys have a seventeenth-century air, with mullioned windows and small leaded panes, while the hotel, owned since 1969 by the entertainers Roy and Jackie Toadoff, with its three-tiered double bays has an Edwardian elegance, as a result of rebuilding.

In the bar of the inn there is a medieval arch in the party wall and a tunnel ran between the two buildings. Further proof that they were once one building is that they have a common ghost, who turns off the gas cylinders on the beer apparatus in the cellars. The landlord of the *Green Dragon* in 1982, who took over in 1976, reckoned the ghost was a campaigner for real ale as it only switched off the keg cylinders. The manager of the *Chantry*, Stuart Hammond, had other troubles. The lights were switched on and off and the fridge plug pulled out. On one occasion glass from the Welsh dresser flew across the room, though no-one was hurt.

Nothing has happened recently in either place.

Fox House Inn

....

THE INN, which used to be called *The Traveller's Rest*, is right on the Sheffield boundary in South Yorkshire, while the Longshaw Estate over the road is in Derbyshire.

It was originally a shepherd's cottage, built about 1773 by George Fox of Callow Farm. A Stranger's Guide to Sheffield published in 1852 said of the inn, then kept by Mr. Thomas Furness, 'for attention and good accommodation there is no better house on the road.'

The middle section of the inn is the oldest and contains the remains of an earlier

cottage on the site, dating back to about 1930. The lounge was added in 1849 by the Duke of Rutland, together with the rooms above and cellars below. The Duke would stay at the inn with a friend when he was bird watching, being looked after by the landlord and his family instead of by servants.

The public bar was added in 1895. The Carter Milner and Bird brewery, now defunct, bought it from the Duke in 1927.

It was the custom every October for most of the shopkeepers in the Shepherd's Society on Penistone Moors to send their sheep to winter on the East Moors of the Longshaw Estate and fetch them back again in March. The shepherds used to meet at the *Fox House Inn*.

Longshaw is now famous for its sheepdog trials. There is a legend of a tunnel from the cellars of the inn to the Lodge. This may be a distortion of the fact that 150 years ago there was a sort of tunnel through bushes from the Lodge to a gate in the wall opposite the inn, along which the servants could sneak off for a tankard of ale unseen by the Duke.

When the Hayes family moved in in 1973, they had fitted wardrobes put in. For two weeks while the work was in hand, the bed in their son's bedroom was moved from its usual place. Each morning there was a noise like the son had fallen out of bed but he hadn't. The sounds stopped as soon as the bed was moved back. They frequently hear voices in other rooms, even when they know that they are empty, but they can never make out what they say.

Perhaps one of the voices belongs to the faceless monk who walks through the bar. A customer, born in 1908, whose family looked after the inn for forty years, says that they used to have similar experiences.

In recent years there have been seen the ghosts of a child, a woman and a headless body. Once all the tubes were shattered in a sun-bed and a glass flew across the kitchen. In the bedroom known as the ghost's room there is a feeling of an unseen presence. A regular lady guest finds all the buttons on her boots undone by an unknown hand.

Snake Inn

Ashopton Woodlands

························

IN 1818, an Act of Parliament, supported by the Duke of Devonshire, was passed to build a turnpike road from Sheffield to Glossop over the High Peak. It opened to traffic in August 1821. A toll bar was in operation at the *Snake Inn* until 1870. A coach-and-four passenger service was introduced, but the complete journey was too much for one team of horses, so the inn and staging post were built 1,680 feet above sea-level, exactly half-way between Glossop and the *Ashop Hotel* (now under Ladybower Reservoir).

The date 1821, together with the snake crest of the Cavendish family, the Dukes of Devonshire, was incorporated in the original inn sign, which was removed about 1923. So the name did not originate from the tortuousness of the road as is generally believed. Part of the outbuildings and the cottage on the west corner of the inn yard are later additions. The Banqueting Suite extension was built in 1964.

The first licence for the inn was given to the Duke of Devonshire and it remained in the family until it was taken over by the National Trust. It was first let out as a farm and pub at an annual rent of £4 for the pub and £14 for the land to John Longden, a Methodist local preacher, whose family remained there until 1879 when the Rowarths took over.

It is said that the ghost of a nineteenth century prize fighter now haunts the inn, but he has not been seen in recent years.

Strines Inn

Bradfield

························

TO THE WEST of the Strines reservoir amidst lonely moorland lies the *Strines Inn*, once a manor house. It was probably built in the 15th century, though it was first recorded in 1568, by a member of the Worrall family.

It was the seat of the Worrall family for many years, but then owned by the Earl Fitzwilliam. It has long been famous as a centre for the grouse-shooting on the moors. It became an inn in the middle of the nineteenth century.

When the new landlords, Mr S. Harrison and Mr S.R. Holden, moved in in 1982, having bought it from the Wise family who had owned it for over twenty years, they thought that the staff were playing tricks. In the side room downstairs can be seen a pair of brass vases, unremarkable to look at, of unknown age and origin. Over a period of six months the right vase never moved but the left one was regularly found to have moved overnight on the mantlepiece, sometimes just an inch or two, though at times it was even lying on the floor.

At one o'clock one morning Mr Harrison and Mr Holden were entertaining two friends in the upstairs restaurant. Mr Holden decided to go down to the garden to check on the chickens. He was away about five minutes. The door to the stairs was open and it was impossible for him to come back up without his friends hearing him. Yet all three of them distinctly heard footsteps in the upstairs corridor, though there could not have been anyone there. A minute or two later, Mr Holden came in from the garden and back up the stairs.

The ghost still walks in the upstairs dining room, according to Mr J.B. Stanish, landlord from March 1995.

In the early summer of 1995, at about 10.30 one morning, two cleaners and a chef saw a little old lady walking across the upstairs restaurant floor. If anyone is upset, she walks up and down as if she, too, is upset.

Mavis Martin, the bar-lady from 1994, felt a sudden cold atmosphere as if the ghost were walking past. Lady chef, Marie, has seen the old lady's outline in the kitchen.

In the Oak Room there are two plant pots in the fireplace. The same one is regularly found knocked over on a morning.

Grouse and Trout Inn
Redmires

T HIS INN, on the road to Fairthorne Green and up to Stanage Pole, was demolished about 1950, leaving only the old sign made of stone on which was carved a grouse and three trout and the motto *Ich Dien Dinner*. The licence was taken away in 1913, when Mr and Mrs Taylor were landlords, because the owner, Mr William Wilson, of Beauchief Hall, thought that too many people would be tempted to take advantage of the new motor-buses running from Manchester Road to Lodge Moor to visit the pub and then venture on to the nearby grouse

moors, thus ruining his shoot.

However, as the Coffee House, the place still became a favourite stop for ramblers, even though they could only buy tea and other non-alcoholic drinks with their sandwiches. Most folk actually went by tram to Nether Green and walked up to the plain white building.

On Christmas Eve, 1864, when Thomas Lowe was landlord, a stranger came to stay for one night. The next morning he was found dead, with his throat cut and a bloodstained razor nearby.

On Christmas Eve, 1912, a young man walking over the moors from Bamford to Sheffield asked for a night's lodgings. The landlord said he had only one room available and that was reputed to be haunted, but the young man said that ghosts did not worry him.

Early the next morning, he woke early and started to shave. Suddenly the room became colder, and icy fingers gripped his wrist forcing the razor against his throat. For a moment he was terrified, then he started to laugh. He was using a safety razor!

During the building of the Redmires dams, the *Grouse and Trout* had many Irish navvies among its customers. However, it was purchased in 1934 and closed down by the Water Committee of the City Council, who had a policy that all houses and farms in the catchment area of the dams had to be demolished to avoid contamination of the water.

The Peacock Inn
Owler Bar

A MILE PAST TOTLEY as one leaves Sheffield, this fine old coaching inn is situated on the Owler Bar roundabout with the toll bar cottage on its right.

The word 'Owler' is from the alder tree. Perhaps there were more of them in the vicinity in the old days. Now the inn is surrounded by moor land.

The original inn dated from the early sixteenth century, slightly forward of the present building., which was built in 1848 by the Duke of Devonshire. Common lands were enclosed by the Act of 1816 and the Award of 10th November 1820. There were 2650 acres of common land at Holmesfield out of the total parish area of 4600 acres. The fields first enclosed were between Moorwoods Land and the Peacock.

Standing 1010 feet above sea level, the pub/restaurant is built of millstone grit and retains its old-world charm with wooden beams and low ceilings. The lounge has an open fire at one end, and there is another room apart from the restaurant, which seats sixty people. An extension is being built by the new owners Barbara and David Neville. It will eventually have 25 bedrooms, two of which will be suites with four-poster beds, bathrooms, living rooms and jacuzzis.

The previous owners, Alice and Antonio Fernandes regularly saw the White Lady during the twenty years before their retirement at Easter 1997. Judy, the barmaid has also seen her behind the bar and described her as in her early twenties and very beautiful, dressed in a white shroud which showed only her face.

In 1996, the chef, who has been there for twelve years, saw a man in a long frock-coat in the car park in front of the pub. He has also seen a headless man in the dining room. Five monks have also been spotted, walking in single file across the field at the back of the pub, but there are no ghosts of the peacock who strutted in safety around the pub courtyard until the advent of the motor car.

Toll Bar Cottage
Owler Bar

．．．．．．．．．．．．．．．．．．．．．．．．．．．．

THE FIRST TURNPIKE road was built in 1781 and the old toll bar was at Wragg's homestead. The new toll bar and cottage has stood at the road junction by the corner of the pub yard from about 1816-18. The cottage changes hands quite frequently. Curious tales are told, such as the time when one owner got up in the middle of the night to go to the toilet. He returned to his bedroom to find a little old lady about four feet tall and dressed in a Victorian nightgown sleeping in his bed. He turned off the lights and then turned them on again, but she was still there.

The Phoenix Inn
High Lane, Ridgeway

．．．．．．．．．．．．．．．．．．．．．．．．．．．．

ON THE B6054 leading south-east from Sheffield stands this seventeenth century coaching inn, now renovated by Wards brewery without losing its traditional charm – or its ghost.

Then in August 1990, after three months work, it re-opened with the old stable and hayloft incorporated as a raised lounge area with the original beams renovated. An extension was built to the bar area and restaurant, and the kitchens were brought thoroughly up-to-date. Even the toilets now have facilities for babies and disabled people. The conservatory with its beautiful pagoda style roof overlooks a terrace and gardens where customers can sit in the summer.

In the field behind the inn there is said to be a Roman burial ground. Two hundred and fifty years ago a serving-wench was murdered in the field by the then landlord and it is supposed to be she who haunts the cellar and moves glasses.

In the spring of 1992, the manager Dave Holman described how dogs refused to go into the restaurant extension, large pepper mills placed on tables are found a few minutes later on the floor, and chairs apparently move by themselves, The serving-wench is not always so shy however. On one famous occasion she emerged from a wall, which partially divides the old part of the restaurant and the extension, walked straight through a table placed against a wall, where a couple were eating their meal, crossed to the bar, floated through the wall and disappeared. The couple, needless to say, left The Phoenix in a hurry!

Aston Hall Hotel

Worksop Rd, Aston

....

S INCE NOVEMBER 1988 a 28-bedroomed hotel, Aston Hall was designed by the famous York architect, John Carr and built in 1772 for Lord Holderness, Secretary of State for the North, replacing the old mansion of the D'Arcy family on the same site.

The original Hall was one of the seats of the Balguy family, whose residence at Aston and Derwent can be traced for twenty generations from Thomas de Balgi, who in the reign of Edward I married the heiress of the Astons. A Balguy was in Elizabeth I's parliament and another was High Sheriff under Charles II.

Lord Holderness never lived at the Hall but let it to Harry Verelst, former governor of Bengal and assistant to Clive of India. Verelst bought the house in 1774/5 and his family erected the service wing in 1825.

The Lords Byron, father and poet son,

visited the house on different occasions and each ran off with the Current Lady of the Manor. The father took his ladylove to Paris, but his son only took his love to Newstead Abbey, where he changed his mind and sent her back to Aston Hall.

For forty years, it was Aughton Court Hospital, a Rotherham council home for mentally backward ladies. For a short time it was owned by Firth and Pillings, the pharmaceutical company. Several murders took place at the Hall in its early years and there are rumours of a secret passage in a bedroom, found by workers carrying out the hotel conversion.

Since it has been an hotel there have been several strange incidents.

Within four weeks of opening, a receptionist saw a white figure in front of her car late at night. Since then wine bottles have rattled in the cellar and the keys on reception have jangled.

One resident saw a blue flashing light in the corner of his bedroom and a chambermaid twice found the telephone in an empty bedroom had been taken off the hook.

A wine waiter was on his own in the cellar, when a wine bottle suddenly smashed to the floor of its own accord, and on another occasion the night porter saw the misty shape of an old man in Victorian dress in the cellar.

In 1991, bridesmaids saw a wedding bouquet move across the dressing table in an otherwise empty room. They rushed out screaming.

A guest in a bedroom on the top floor saw a man and woman walk past the bedroom window – using a fire-escape which had been removed a year or so previously!

Hospitals

Winter Street Hospital

....

ACROSS THE ROAD from where the University Arts Tower now stands, the Borough Hospital for Infectious Diseases, having cost £20,000 to build, opened in 1887 with eighty-four beds.

From 1912, Winter Street Hospital was used for the treatment of consumptives, and except for 1914-19, when it was used as a military hospital, it continued as a TB sanatorium until 1969, when it became a geriatric hospital. In 1976 it was upgraded and re-opened as St. George's Hospital, taking the name of the surrounding parish.

The hospital used to be haunted by a lady dressed in grey. A lady who was a patient there from January to March, 1956 occupied a bed in what became Medical Ward 2. She described how many of the nurses would not go into the ward at night. When a patient needed attention, they would send another nurse who did not mind, or did not believe in ghosts. The lady said that once or twice it felt as if someone was sitting on the bottom of the bed, making the mattress sink. Eventually the mattress went up again, as if someone had just got up again. Yet there was no-one there. Many a night she lay with the sheets pulled over her face, afraid that by the green night-lights she would see a shadowy figure in grey.

One morning the woman by the sluice door was found lying face down in her bed, too scared to move. During the night an unseen hand had pulled the bedclothes up over her shoulders and then the sluice door had opened by itself and closed again.

Renovations and the building of a new section in the early 1980s apparently drove the Grey Lady away.

For a while the hospital took in no patients, being used only for administrative purposes. From 1996, the old day hospital became the St. George's community health centre, and next door has been bought for the University Bartholme House School of Nursing.

Only the sinister-looking gargoyles on the tops of the drainpipes, representing winged mythical creatures such as a dragon, cat, rat, lion, gryphon, dog, Pegasus, owl and pig, remind us of past horrors.

Royal Infirmary

Infirmary Road
....

THE HOSPITAL was opened in 1797. The main building was closed in 1980, with its maze of tunnels in the basement, where the Grey Lady so terrified a porter that he quit his job.

Sister Garrett saw the Grey Lady on Ward 22, as did Harvey Kane one Halloween at 11 am near the service lift, a transparent figure in an old-fashioned nurse's uniform. She is reputed on one occasion to have given medicine to an unsuspecting patient.

The newer buildings, too, eventually closed and some were demolished. Safeway built a supermarket on part of the site, the old entrance lodge became a shop, now closed, selling ski equipment to skiers on the nearby artificial ski slope, and Norwich Union retained the old Central Block – which is a listed building – the Round House and the old nurses' home, Centenary House, built in 1897. A new block has been built alongside, in a similar style of architecture, to house their headquarters, which opened in September 1989.

The Grey Lady happily accepted the changes and was frequently seen by the staff of Norwich Union.

Part of Safeway is built over the old mortuary. One night soon after the supermarket opened, the alarm connected to the local police station went off. Officers investigating saw at the back of the store two figures dressed in white, who mysteriously vanished. There was no sign of a break in.

Firvale Infirmary and City General Hospital (Northern General)

Barnsley Road
....

NOW PART of Northern General Hospital, the foundation stone for the new combined hospital and work-house was laid on 6th September 1878 on the site of Hagg farmhouse, owned by Mr George Clark, and it was officially opened in 1881.

In the main building were 1,800 paupers, with separate asylums to the south for 200 more. Where St. Luke's Chapel now stands was a school for 200 children. The hospital had 366 beds and there was a separate Fever Hospital. The vagrants' ward took 60 men and 20 women.

Casual quarters were separate from the rest of the workhouse. On admission everyone had to strip and bathe and put on a dark woollen nightdress and were given some rugs. They were then locked in a small cell furnished only with a large plank for a bed, with a raised box-like end for a pillow. There was a tiny inner cell where stone-breaking was done and the broken stone thrown out through a grating.

Men were given up to 13 cwt. (550 kilos) of stone to break, less of the harder stone, or to pick 41b. of unbeaten or 81b. of beaten oakum, or nine hours digging, pumping, sawing wood or grinding. Women did half the amount of oakum or nine hours washing, scrubbing or needlework, making the ugly uniforms. The infirm old women looked after the infants.

Casual workers, wandering from town to town in search of work, received half the amount of food as a regular inmate, bread and gruel for breakfast, bread and cheese for dinner and bread and gruel for supper. The paupers had milk porridge and bread for supper and breakfast, and for dinner, boiled beef and potatoes, fish, pea-meal soup or hash.

There was no tea for those under 60, but at Firvale they were fortunate to get coffee twice on Sundays and once on Thursdays. Black beetles were an unwelcome flavouring. Unmarried men who came in each day just to work got 9d (4p) a day (3d in bread, one penny in tea, one penny in sugar and 4d in money to pay for a night's lodging).

After 1890 there were many improvements: a less starchy diet more suitable for manual workers; skilled artisans were not put to stonebreaking or other work which would make them unfit to do their proper work; there were more trained nurses in the hospital; outworkers received the normal rate of pay for the district and there were married quarters for old couples who had previously been separated.

A separate hospital block was built in 1902-6, called Sheffield Union Hospital, with 643 beds. It gradually became better known as Firvale Hospital. Originally it was only for the workhouse inmates, but eventually took more and more outsiders who were able to pay. It was a general hospital but had no out-patient or casualty departments.

In 1914, the new children's hospital opened, but at first was used for wounded soldiers. Labour and maternity units were in the old children's hospital.

In 1930 Sheffield City Council took over from the Board of Guardians and the hospital was re-named the City General Hospital. Firvale House was transferred to the Public Assistance Committee of the Council and re-named Firvale Infirmary.

The City General had its first out-patient clinic in 1945. There were still wards for vagrants, taking between 60 and 90 a night on behalf of the National Assistance Board and later the Social Care Department.

In April 1967, Firvale with 682 beds for geriatrics, and the City General with 654 beds, amalgamated and the Firvale wards ceased to be known by the names of poets and were given numbers.

The Grey lady of Firvale is a woman who nursed there in the 1880s, and is still to be met with today. In the winter of 1971 a nurse at the Northern General finished her shift at 9 pm, leaving a few minutes later than usual, so that as she walked down Firvale Drive, there was no-one to accompany her. She was pleased to see someone ahead of her wearing what appeared to be a long maxi-coat. The person kept ahead of her until they had passed the turn-off to Barnsley Road. Then suddenly the person vanished. The nurse stopped and looked round, but there was no place she could have gone to. It was only the following day at work that the nurse learned about the Grey Lady.

The geriatric block had other unofficial residents. In 1982, a young boy and girl in Victorian nightclothes drifted up to nursing staff on a certain ward late one night. When the nurses spoke to them, they disappeared. The following night, a shadowy figure was seen in what was supposed to be an empty bed. A nurse, investigating, found that the bed was empty but very cold to her touch.

In 1985, a kitchen was closed down at night after staff were unnerved by an incident which occurred when nursing and other staff were taking a late-night tea-break in the first floor dining-room. One female member of the catering staff was working alone in the basement kitchen. The staff upstairs were horrified to hear a loud scream and the clatter of pots and pans being hurled around. They ran down, expecting to find that there had been an accident, but everything was in its place and the woman was cheerfully at work, having heard nothing.

In Wards 37 and 38, which are geriatric wards, in the Northern General there was said to be a ghost called Tommy, who opened and closed the doors.

In the Cardiac Department there used to be a consultant named James Brown, now dead. His ghost has been seen there and people have smelt his tobacco smoke. On one occasion a set of notes went missing. Then as a member of staff walked down an aisle amongst the medical records, the notes were seen sticking out with the name clearly shown. James Brown had found them for them.

On Florence Nightingale Ward, pots and pans jumped around in the kitchen and a chaplain was brought in to perform an exorcism. The Grey Lady has been seen walking on the bridge to the old part of the hospital near Ward 21.

In the Renal Ward in about 1980 there was a sudden cold and a banging on the window as if the bough of a tree was being blown against it, but there was no bough. The patients were evacuated for one night.

Middlewood Hospital

···

I T WAS NOT UNTIL 1818 that the first public asylum in the West Riding was built at Wakefield. It soon became overcrowded as a result of the increase in population and the stresses of the newly urbanised communities which could not absorb people with mental problems as easily as rural communities. The 1834 Poor Law Amendment Act provided for special wards in workhouses for the care of the mentally sick, but the most dangerous were transferred within fourteen days to the County Asylum.

As Wakefield Asylum was inadequate, it was decided to buy land at Wadsley Park from the Countess of Bute to build a new asylum with 400 beds. The land had formerly been part of the estate of the Earl of Wharncliffe.

Meanwhile, Mount Pleasant House at the London Road end of Sharrow Lane was leased in 1868 for five years at an annual rent of £350, and 68 female and 6 male patients were transferred from Wakefield.

At Wadsley, land was levelled and building commenced in the summer of 1869. The South Yorkshire Asylum was opened on 27th August 1872, with seven patients from Wakefield.

Larger than originally planned, it had 750 beds and cost £150,714. It had its own bakery, brewery for beer (each patient had half-a-pint a day, one pint if working), laundry and workshops. The sick and infirm were on the ground floors, the dayrooms were on the middle floors and the dormitories on the top floors.

Just outside the city boundary until 1974, it was actually administered from Wakefield until 1948. Its catchment area included Sheffield, Ecclesall Bierlow, Rotherham, Doncaster, Thorne, Penistone, Wortley and part of Worksop. It cost the Poor Law Authorities 10/6d a week (just over 50 pence) to maintain each patient, including medicines, food, clothes, bedding and wages. There were a few private patients, who were charged £1 a week.

The asylum church was completed in 1875 for £6,000. After an outbreak of dysentry in 1876 due to overcrowding of the 1,089 patients, two additional blocks were built within two years on the 163-acre estate. The main lodge was built in 1878 and the nurses' home in 1893, so freeing many single bedrooms for more patients.

In 1895 was built the Isolation Hospital for intestinal infections. It later became the Male Detached Infirmary and was later the Hillside Geriatric Unit. In 1914 the separate admissions block on Middlewood Road was built for £60,000.

From January 1915 to July 1920, as the Wharncliffe War Hospital with 1,500 beds, it cared for 35,000 soldiers. The mental patients were sent to other hospitals. Afterwards, 300 beds were kept as a

Ministry of Pensions hospital.

The 'Bungalow' TB sanatorium was built in 1928. In 1929, the Wadsley Asylum was renamed the West Riding Mental Hospital, Wadsley, and in 1935 the new admissions hospital was named 'The Middlewood Hospital', to distinguish it from the main hospital. The Occupational Therapy Unit dates from 1936.

In 1939, the Emergency Medical Services took over the whole of the male detached block and part of the female detached block. This Wharncliffe Emergency Hospital dealt with medical, surgical and neurosis casualties, especially after Dunkirk and D-day.

In 1946 the National Health Service Act integrated mental health services with general health and social services, and so in 1948 the newly-named Middlewood Hospital (which now included all wards, not just the admissions block,) was placed under the Sheffield Regional Hospital Board when the West Riding Mental Hospitals Board was dissolved.

Since 1957 there was much modernisation and new units were built, including the industrial workshop from 1961, which carried out sub-contracts for local firms. In 1956, however, the farm and dairy herd were discontinued as being unnecessary for occupational therapy. There were over 2,000 patients, despite extensive rehabilitation into the community.

It is not surprising that the highly-charged emotional atmosphere which can surround mentally disturbed patients should retain the images of past events.

In the summer of 1976, between twelve midnight and one o'clock, a nurse and nursing officer were seated in the Admissions Ward. The fire-door was barred but not locked. It suddenly flew open by itself.

On Ward 12 a nurse made a ouija board and played with it with a young male student. The board definitely spun round. Unfortunately, they did not break the glass afterwards, which probably explains the

mysterious happenings which began from that time on the ward. The spirit called up by the ouija board was still imprisoned on this earthly plane. There were stairs up at one side and mysterious footsteps were heard going up and stopping at the top.

Ward 13 had been redecorated, but as yet there were no patients and furniture. One night at one-thirty, a male student nurse, a female nurse and a nursing officer heard a loud noise. The nursing officer, a big chap, and the student went up to look.

The outer door to the fire-escape was open, but otherwise there was nothing to be seen in the empty room. A nurse from Ward 11 came along, and when the men had gone the other nurse took her up. The men had closed the outer door, but it was again swinging open. Afterwards the nurses were instructed not to investigate strange noises alone.

In Ward 8 upstairs, at least two nurses at separate times while on night duty in the early 1970s, saw an old woman in a nightie, who turned and walked away from them through the wall. Perhaps it was the same old lady whom another nurse saw. She told her to get back into bed. The old lady took no notice but went on up the corridor.

The nurse went after her, thinking that she was not wearing the regulation nightdress, and made to touch her on the shoulder. The woman turned. Under her light-coloured night-cap she had no face!

On Ward 1 a female nurse and a student saw a patient climbing out over the bottom of his bed at the far end of the ward. They went to stop him and found him dead in bed. Presumably they had seen his spirit leaving his body.

On the mixed Hillside Ward, since pulled down, the same nurse, a sister and a student were on duty one night when a male patient collapsed and died. The body was put on a trolley in the bathroom until it could be taken to the mortuary in the morning.

The patient had had the habit of knocking on his locker. Although no other patient was awake, all through the rest of that night, wrecking the nerves especially of the first-year male student, a sound was heard in the ward as of a continual knocking on a locker!

Just before the wards were renovated, a minister of religion was brought in to exorcise them, and afterwards the numbers were changed round so that no-one ward would gain notoriety. Only time would tell how successful was the exorcism.

The hospital was gradually closed down by 1996, demolished and the grounds sold off for housing, with due regard for the preservation of the ancient fossilised trees.

Nether Edge Hospital

···

B OUNDED BY Lyndhurst Rd, Union Road and Osborne Road, it was mainly closed down by 2000, and some original buildings have since been demolished.

The earliest known workhouse in Sheffield was listed by William Fairbank, surveyor to the Marquis of Rockingham, Lord of the Manor in 1761. Samuel Naw's two houses and his Homestead were used as a workhouse for the Ecclesall Liberty at Cherry Tree Hill.

The workhouse on Psalter Lane, then Sharrow Moor, had accomodation for 60-80 people. In January 1839 the Board of Guardians decided it was inadequate and bought land at Nether Edge to build a larger one. In 1845 the old workhouse was sold to Henry Newbould of Sharrow House for £1200.

The new workhouse was built under the auspices of the new Ecclesall-Bierlow Union formed by the Poor Law

Commissioners in 1837. A stone building in Elizabethan style, it cost £9,000 to build. It opened in 1843.

In 1905, the Fulwood Cottage Homes for children opened, costing £8,143. In 1898-9, the infirmary was opened for 104 male patients. A maternity hospital with 12 beds cost £2,400.

In 1912, it was proposed to use the workhouse hospital exclusively for surgical and medical cases and to build a sanatorium for consumptives.

In 1925, the two unions of Sheffield and Ecclesall-Bierlow were dissolved and the Sheffield Union was set up. By 1929 relief of the poor was not the responsibility of the Sheffield Union but that of the Sheffield City Council Public Assistance Committee.

In 1929 the Institution became known as Nether Edge Hospital. The term 'workhouse' had been abandoned in 1914.

The original architect was William Flockton (1804-64), son of a carpenter and builder of Rockingham Street.

The accomodation was for 500 people, including 44 boys and 44 girls. By 1905 there were 1037 inmates, with an average of 100 vagrants a week. A national survey in 1866-8 of 48 provincial workhouses discovered that 38% of the paupers were sick. The generally sick were not separated from infectious cases in workhouse hospitals.

At Nether Edge there were many new wards built in the 1960s and 1970s – for elderly acutely ill patients, maternity and gynaecology, a stroke unit, rheumatology (when the Edgar Allen centre was closed) and a day hospital.

In 1989, Sheffield Health Authority, reviewing all hospitals, decided, because of these new buildings, to keep Nether Edge and to close Lodge Moor. In 1990 it merged with the Royal Hallamshire and Jessops Hospital for Women to form Central Sheffield University Hospitals. In 1992 this became a NHS Trust.

Nether Edge, spread over 18 acres, had increasing problems. Many buildings were sub-standard and underused. Derelict buildings were demolished and car parks extended. However, it was eventually decided that only the west part of the site with Cavendish and Lyndhurst blocks, a psychiatric outpatient unit and a 93-bed in-patient unit for the mentally ill would be kept. The rest would be sold off to developers, mainly for housing.

Like most hospitals Nether Edge has its ghostly legends. A recent one concerns footsteps heard running across the roof of Sheaf block, even though the door to the roof is kept looked. They have been heard at various times by different people. It is said that at New Year 1994, a young man who had been working on the top floor was celebrating too hard. He managed to get up onto the roof, where, completely drunk, he fell over the edge and was killed.

Other eerie sounds may originate from the days of the Second World War, when 143 London evacuees were given temporary shelter. In December 1940 the hospital was hit by three high-explosive bombs and many incendiaries. Neal Ward, the dining hall, store-rooms and a nurses' home were all lost.

The Royal Hospital

West Street

······································

THE CHOLERA EPIDEMIC of 1831 led to the opening of a Dispensary to supply poor people with simple remedies, first aid dressings, ointments and pills. It was situated on the site of the present Central Library in a house belonging to a Mr Dawson, rented for £30 a year. However, it soon became necessary to find larger premises and Westfield House on West Street, the former home of a Mr Bailey was bought in December 1832 for £1,300. The Town Trustees gave a grant of £100.

The necessity to build wards for in-patients was soon apparent. A small casualty and operating ward from which patients could be sent home immediately, which opened in 1852, was clearly inadequate.

A General Hospital was built in 1859, but owing to a lack of money, it did not open until 12th April 1860. There were twenty-one beds, together with the dispensary, but it soon had to be enlarged in 1869. In 1871 there were 100 beds, but from lack of funds only 70 were in use. The accounts for the first six months of 1871 showed 727 gallons of ale, 1392 bottles of porter and 252 gallons of beer were consumed!

In 1875, when maternity cases went to the Women's Hospital in Fig Tree Lane, the Sheffield Public Hospital was recognised as a teaching hospital by the Royal College of Surgeons.

Eventually it was decided to demolish all the old buildings and adjoining buildings were bought up, so that an enlarged hospital could be built. The last old building was pulled down in 1906.

The Royal Hospital was opened by the Duke and Duchess of York on 11th May, 1895. It gradually expanded until by 1900 it extended from Westfield Terrace to Eldon Street. A central block of five wards was built in 1902 and a nurses' home in Eldon Street in 1896. During the First World War two wards were used for wounded soldiers.

In 1922, Mount Zion Chapel was bought to be converted into an outpatients' department for £9,000. Opened by Neville Chamberlain in 1927, it had been built in 1834 and, as a listed building it is the only survivor of the Royal Hospital, which was closed down in 1978. The other buildings were demolished in 1981.

The Zion Chapel was bought by the Northern Counties Housing Association for their Sheffield regional office. The original facade has been retained and renovated.

Like most hospitals the Royal had its legends, notably the Grey Lady, a former nurse. Unnerving incidents are recorded. Two lady visitors were quite prepared to believe in the supernatural when the lift they were in stopped between floors and the lights went out. It restarted itself after a minute or so and the lights went on again.

Ghosts in Schools

The Brushes

Formerly Firth Park Comprehensive School, Barnsley Road

....

LONG BEFORE Brush House was built by John Booth in the 1790s there was a Brushes Farm four hundred yards down the road to Sheffield on the edge of Brushes Common.

During the Civil War the farm was owned by the Cavalier, Captain Burley. While he was away fighting, his house keeper Anne Warter and two servants fought off several attacks from June 13th-18th, 1646. Burley was executed in 1646 on the Isle of Wight. The Roundheads seized the farm and sold it to Emanuel Scorah. In 1700, Frances Scorah sold it to William Motte, who sold it to John Booth of Loundside, who also bought Whitley Farm in 1712.

His son, John Booth, inherited the farm

in 1726 and was also a nailer. He later made a fortune in iron and steel when he went into partnership with Aaron and Samuel Walker, building a steel furnace at Masbrough in 1748. In 1750 he signed a twenty-one year agreement with John Roebuck (later of the Carron Iron Works, Scotland, in partnership with James Watt).

John Booth III, the grandson, retained the old farmhouse alongside Barnsley Road, but removed the farm buildings. He built a large new house on the east side of the old one. Until recently, when the school moved to a new site, this was the main part of the school building. The other house was later demolished by the Kaysers of the steel firm of Kayser Ellison, who were of German origin, to make room for the Tower.

Though empty now, the science block stands on the site of the old farmhouse. Booth enclosed Brushes Common in 1784 and laid out beautiful gardens and plantations, where Firth Park housing estate was built in 1922-4. A scientist and philosopher, Booth quarrelled with the Vicar of Ecclesfield over a game of cards, and vowed not to be buried in the churchyard. He built his own mausoleum, consecrated by the Archbishop of York, where he was buried with his favourite horse. In 1921 a council workman found a vault with their skeletons at the top of the Oval Wood. The mausoleum was destroyed and the human remains transferred to Burngreave Cemetery in 1922, together with the original stones, now disappeared, inscribed *Eximius vir Johannes Booth hic placide iacet.*

The Oval Road of today is the true shape and size of the grim, dark, Haunted Wood. At the north-west end the large square vault had a stone obelisk at each corner, one of which became an ornament in a nearby garden. The whole wood was enclosed by a drystone wall eight feet high and topped with ivy, which still stands along Barnsley Road.

It was said to be haunted by Captain Booth on his white charger. Mrs Charles Kayser was once terrified by the sight of them 'near the big tree in front of the Mausoleum'. In recent years school cleaners claim to have seen, from the library wing, mysterious movements in that direction.

The Booths, who had on occasion leased the house to members of the local gentry, sold it in 1888 to the Kaysers, who in turn left it for Endcliffe Grange in 1903. Then it was sold to Sheffield Corporation by Miss Jane Wake, who had no heirs.

The first pupils at Firth Park Secondary School moved in in September 1920. By 1923 there were 323 boys at the Brushes and 168 at Abbeyfield House, Pitsmoor. They all came together at the Brushes in 1927 and Abbeyfield became a public library, after ten more classrooms, an assembly hall, gym and laboratory had been added to the Brushes.

In 1937, when a library, art room and six more classrooms were added, the school was re-named Firth Park Grammar School. In 1969, it became a comprehensive school, amalgamating with Hatfield House Lane Secondary Modern mixed school, 1,200 children altogether.

Today it is difficult to sift fact from fiction among the ghostly tales passed on from one generation of pupils to the next. One master, who shall be nameless, admitted that he himself had spun some of the tales to the credulous innocents in his class.

One legend is a variation on the horseman story, in which Mary Booth used to meet her horseman lover in what is now Longley Park. They were caught one night by Mary's husband, who killed the horseman. Mary later hung herself, and is buried at Longley Park, through which a ghostly horseman is said to ride on St. Valentines Day.

However, the unhappy Mary is not to be found in the Booth family tree printed in

Teachers were strangely reticent about a practical joke that misfired when the real ghost appeared. In addition, a poltergeist amused itself by overturning chairs, displacing books, and switching on lights in empty, locked rooms, while glass broke of its own accord in a laboratory.

Another story concerns the 'Blue Lady'. A maid, Hanaly Smith, was murdered in Room 2. The butler was blamed and hanged himself in the Tower. It was later proved that the son of the house was responsible. The assistant caretaker had smelled violets and lavender, though she had not seen the Blue Lady.

Firth Park could not be called a dull school!

Since 1969 the school was on a split site, but in the late 1990s building work began to bring all the pupils together on the Fircroft site at Shiregreen, and that is where they now are, in splendid new and refurbished buildings. The Brushes building will eventually be sold, as it is now in a very bad condition.

The retired school registrar, Rita Fletcher, and the ghost whose lavender-scented perfume she has smelt will miss the crowds of schoolchildren at the Brushes.

The Brushes Story by Mr T.F. Johnson, an ex-history master. An enquiry at Longley Park Lodge revealed that the 'gravestone' in a culvert by the stream is not for Mary Booth, but is a seventeenth-century memorial to plague victims. Needless to say, the news of a ghostly horseman was received with much hilarity.

The Tower was kept locked to prevent pupils hunting the ghost of one of the Booths – not a schoolboy who hung himself! – which manifests itself as an indeterminate presence. There are other permanent residents, an old maidservant and a lady in grey who walk the halls and corridors.

Myers Grove School
Wood Lane
....

MYERS GROVE SCHOOL opened in 1960 to serve lower Stannington, Walkley and parts of Malin Bridge. For almost thirty years it took pupils from ages eleven to eighteen, but then it lost its sixth form. It is now on one site in Wood Lane between the rivers Loxley and Rivelin and Loxley College now occupies what used to be Myers Grove lower school. The area around the school used to be called Woodlands and consisted mainly of playing fields. A local man was employed to mow the grass and liked his job so much that even after his death and despite the fact that school buildings now cover most of the site, he continues to mow the grass. At night, it is said, one can still hear the sound of his lawn-mower around Loxley College.

Wisewood School

Rural Lane

WISEWOOD SCHOOL opened in 1933 as Wisewood High School, on the edge of the countryside overlooking Loxley valley, taking about 660 pupils aged eleven to sixteen. In 1969, a comprehensive school was built down the road and pupils transferred to it. The infant and junior schools are now in Ben Lane.

Until 1979, pupils had to be bussed to Marlcliffe Junior School, a mile away for some lessons.

There was an eighteenth-century cottage where the craft block now stands. It was demolished about 1970. John Hunter, who used to live there, said that at night he would hear mysterious footsteps going up the stairs.

The ghost, it seems, has now made the school its home. In 1992 the caretaker, Jim Whitham, said that he had heard ghostly footsteps crossing the upstairs maths corridor. Both he and assistant caretaker Mick Riley heard the sounds of doors slamming after all the doors were locked, and after all the lights were switched off at night, they saw them come on again by themselves. Mr Riley had heard and seen the figure of a man walking up and down on the roof.

There is a phone in the caretaker's house which is connected with the phone in the school office. When the receiver is picked up a red light comes on. Mr Whitham saw this light come on at weekends, when there was no-one in the school.

Holt House

Abbeydale Road

APPROPRIATELY, 'holt' means 'wooded hill'. There has been a Holt House on the site since the sixteenth century, perhaps even earlier.

The manor of Ecclesall was created at the beginning of the thirteenth century and Radolphus de Ecclesall settled there. He gave the monks of Beauchief Abbey his corn mill at Millhouses and land on the banks of the River Sheaf. He also built a chapel for which the monks were to supply a priest.

In 1343, the manor passed to the Scrope family. In 1534, John Scheffeld, last abbot of Beauchief, leased to Richard Jeystock, his son Robert and daughter-in-law

Catherine 'one tenement, lands, meadow and pasture within the Byerlow of Ecclesall, which tenement is called Hoolt House, for thirty years', for a rent of twenty shillings and extra at spring and harvest.

Later in the sixteenth century, after passing to Sir Nicholas Strelley and then to the Pegge family, it belonged to William Matthew of Sheffield, who in 1713 sold it to John Bright of Chesterfield. One of his descendants married Charles, last Marquis of Rockingham in 1752, the estate thus becoming part of the Fitzwilliam estates.

By the 1779 Enclosure Act – 'for dividing and enclosing several open commons, moors and waste ground in the Manor and Township of Ecclesall' – about 1,000 acres, the Holt House estate, was divided into several tenancies.

In 1806, Holt House was owned by Joseph Wilson, Esquire, and in 1834 by John Rodgers, who later built Abbeydale Grange.

The 1869 edition of *Hunter's Hallamshire* said that Holt House had recently been re-built on the same site by its owner, John Firth, merchant and manufacturer.

In 1918, the three-storeyed house was sold by the Firths to Sheffield Education Committee to become part of Abbeydale Girls' Grammar School. The Holt House Infant School, which opened in 1954, was in an entirely new building nearby.

From 1981, Holt House was the head office of Sheaf Valley Adult Education Division.

Mrs Atkinson, who attended Hurfield Grammar School in the war years, recalled how war was declared a few days before the autumn term of 1939 was due to start, so the school was closed and the army took over, using the playing fields for drilling. Teachers took classes for small groups of children in private houses during Home Service, which was deemed safer in case of air raids. After six months of 'phoney' war, however, the schools opened normally.

One day, during a lesson in the room adjoining the balcony, the later Mrs Atkinson, larking around, leaned backwards in her chair and overbalanced, falling against the wooden panelling. To her astonishment the panelling slid back and girl and chair fell into a concealed cupboard, empty and quite narrow, being about five foot high. Unfortunately, when the caretaker, Mr Steve Day investigated, he found evidence that panelling and cupboards had been removed from various rooms over the years.

He recalled being present in 1974 when the tunnel from the Holt House cellars to Beauchief Abbey was blocked up as it was in a dangerous condition.

There is a legend of a maidservant, who, finding herself pregnant, threw herself over the balcony. She is not the only apparition. A cleaning lady entered the conservatory in time to see a white-robed monk rise out of the solid stone floor. Needless to say, the cleaning lady refused to work there again. The previous caretaker's dog would never enter the conservatory.

Holt House was boarded up, but in June 1994 it was set on fire. Unfortunately it was not a listed building and has since been pulled down.

Abbeydale Grange
Abbeydale Road
·······································

ABBEYDALE GRANGE is first mentioned in connection with John Rodgers, a leading member of the firm of Joseph Rodgers, who was living in Abbeydale Road in 1856. According to his tombstone in Ecclesall churchyard, he was 'of Abbeydale House' when he died in 1859, aged eighty years.

According to the 1861 Directory, the

occupant then was Robert Newbold, merchant and manufacturer. *Hunter's Hallamshire* says 'In Abbeydale there is a chaste mansion erected by the late John Rodgers for his own habitation. It is now the property of his nephew who occupies it.' Unfortunately we do not know the exact date of its construction.

From 1881-1910 the house was occupied by Wilson Mappin, director of the Sheffield Gas Company. It was bought from the Firth family in 1918 by the Sheffield Education Committee to house Abbeydale Girls' Secondary School (later Abbeydale Grammar School) until the new building was erected in 1939. (That was damaged in the Blitz, together with the air raid shelters, so that the pupils had to join High Storrs School for a while).

The Grange then became part of Hurlfield Girls' Grammar School, which was then a year old, sharing a building with the Arbourthorne Central Junior School. As its numbers grew, it took over the Grange, Holt House and an old wooden hall. In 1947 new additional prefabricated buildings (supposedly temporary, but still in use!) were put up on the Holt House estate, and the whole of Hurlfield Grammar School came together there. The gym and assembly hall were erected in 1952.

From September 1954 the school's name was changed to the Grange Grammar School. In 1969 it joined with Abbeydale Boys' Grammar School and Abbeydale Girls' Grammar School to become Abbeydale Grange Comprehensive School.

Grange House, now part of Northern College, was the sixth form centre, but became redundant when the sixth form was abolished.

The Grange was listed and so boarded up. Substantial redevelopment was not allowed. After a suspicious fire, it was demolished. What happened to the lady in white who walked in and out of rooms on the upper floor searching for her child?

Handsworth First School
Fitzalan Road
....

HANDSWORTH COUNCIL SCHOOL was built in 1894, but the daily diary written up each day by Headmasters dates back only to 1903. At first it took children from the age of five up to fifteen, but from 1954 it accepted boys and girls from the age of four to eight, and was renamed Handworth First School.

During the Second World War there were plans to use it as a hospital but nothing came of it, although as with other schools it was closed for several months at the beginning of the War when its pupils were taught on Home Service. Huts were added when the school was at its largest, but these are now used for various community projects. From the summer of 1984 it housed Handworth Public Library, after the old library building in Hall Road was declared unsafe and demolished.

The Library staff experienced strange goings-on in their new home. In the Junior Library upstairs, books fell from the shelves for no apparent reason and the staff never felt alone there. It was as if someone was looking in from the corridor windows, even when no-one was there. Was it the ghostly lady, who used to be seen quite regularly downstairs in the Adult Library? On Monday 14th October 1985 a member of staff could scarcely believe her eyes when the date stamp suddenly changed from the 14th to the 2nd and 1985 to 1995 and back again within a few seconds.

Was something destined to happen on 2nd October 1995?

Handworth First School closed in July 1992, its 40 pupils going to Athelstan and Ballifield.

Brook Comprehensive School

Richmond Road
....

THE AREA AROUND Sheffield, in the territory of the Brigantes and Coritani tribes, was sparsely populated in pre-Roman times. Domesday first records the settlement of Handswerde (Handsworth), which before the Conquest was held by the Saxon Torchil and valued at forty shillings. Afterwards it passed to the De Lovetots, then the Furnivals, Talbots and Howards.

Richmond, a separate settlement from Handsworth, was held in the Middle Ages by William of Crespnil, who paid an annual rent of five shillings to the canons of Worksop.

In 1379 there were 13 smiths and three cutlers in Handsworth parish, more than in Sheffield. A brook, perhaps used to power a cutler's grindstone, still runs below Richmond College.

In 1805, Richmond contained twenty houses, grouped along both sides of Richmond Road. A toll-gate stood at the junction with Handsworth Road.

In 1811 the population of Handsworth parish was 1424. Until this century it remained largely agricultural. Gradually Sheffield expanded, but only since 1946 was there large scale building near Brook Secondary Modern School, which opened in January 1954 with 200 boys and girls.

From Autumn 1954 there were 600. In 1966 it became Brook Comprehensive School. In 1974 the first Woodthorpe pupils attended and it had its first sixth-form pupils.

The ghost of the school dining room was first seen about 1971 by the then caretaker and his wife and later by Mrs. Bamforth, a pupil's mother. Jasper always leaves a faint smell of cigar smoke. He was a joiner, who worked on the school. When the first caretaker retired, Jasper wanted the job. When he did not get it he was heartbroken.

Although it had a fine record for academic achievement, the school lost the numbers battle for survival under tertiary reorganisation and was absorbed by Stradbroke Tertiary College in September 1988. The Brook School building now lies empty and vandalised.

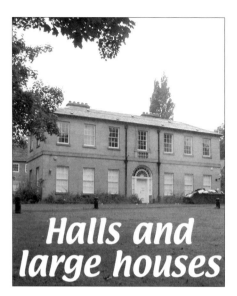

Halls and large houses

Many old houses acquire a reputation for being haunted, often with justification.

Broom Hall

Broomhall Road
....

T HE 'BROM' ESTATE, extending from Crookesmoor to Sheffield Castle over wild moorland covered in broom as well as gorse and heather, was in 1329 settled on Joan de Wanton on her marriage, thus passing to the Wickersleys, a powerful family, who were co-founders with Richard de Busli of Roche Abbey.

Broom Hall was built during the reign of Edward IV (1461-1483) and was in the Wickersley family until 1528, when the last male Wickersley died, leaving a daughter, who married Robert Swyft, principal agent for the fifth Earl of Shrewsbury, President of the Council of the North, and one of the twelve Capital Burgesses of Sheffield.

They made Broom Hall their main residence because of its proximity to the Castle, the Earl's seat. They had only daughters. The youngest married Richard Jessop of Rotherham, who thus acquired Broom Hall and North Lees Hall, Derbyshire.

Francis Jessop was one of a group of enthusiastic observers of natural phenomena, which included Willoughby, who acknowledged in the preface to his *Ornithologiae* that Jessop sent specimens of rare birds found in Sheffield, having lived at Broom Hall from 1641.

Jessop's grandson, James Wilkinson, Vicar of Sheffield (1754-1805) and a JP lived at Broom Hall from 1743. A legendary character known as 'Father of the Town of Sheffield', he was both greatly loved by some and hated by others.

In 1791 there was a riot against the hard conditions of the times and the harshness of the sentences pronounced by Wilkinson as JP. A mob marched on Broom Hall to burn it to the ground. Calling the vicar 'Old Serpent' and 'Black, diabolical fiend', they managed only to destroy some books in the library. It was easier to burn all the haystacks at the rear of the house.

According to the rhyme:

'They burned his books,
And scared his rooks,
And set his stacks on fire.'

Then a company of dragoons from Nottingham arrived and arrested five of the men. The leader, a half-wit named Bennett, was hanged at York Tyburn.

A bachelor, Wilkinson left Broom Hall to a relation, Philip Gell of Hopton, who sold it in 1826 to John Watson of Shirecliffe Hall. Until then the house had been in a beautiful rural, richly cultivated, wooded setting. From 1829, the 104 acres of the estate were covered by high-class housing and Broom Hall itself was divided up and let to two and later three tenants. One part became a farmhouse and another, in 1834, was George Wilkinson's gentlemen's boarding school.

The original building, framed in solid oak, whose H-shaped plan can still be traced, was under William Jessop (1580-1630) largely remodelled, and much of the timber work clad in stone. The centre portion had been built in the reign of Henry VIII (1509-1547) and the east wing added about 1784 in good provincialised Robert Adam style.

However, the nineteenth century and a succession of tenants and misguided alterations led to its deterioration. The Georgian part, the last to be occupied, was used as offices and the interior of the timber part fell into ruins. In 1971, the whole place was abandoned to vandals.

In the 1970s, most of the Broomhall Park estate with its substantial stone-built Victorian houses set in large and pleasant gardens was designated a Conservation area, but the future of Broom Hall itself, one of the very few examples of half-timbered building around Sheffield, was uncertain.

Sheffield Council decided that it could not afford to acquire and restore it. Two separate applications to build an office block in the grounds (one involved partial demolition of the Hall) were refused.

In 1973 it was brought by Mr David Mellor, silversmith and industrial designer. Planning permission was given for a residential and studio-workshop use, the former in the oldest part and the workshop in the Georgian part. The cutlery workshop conversion won the Architectural Heritage Year Award. Its products sold around the world, helping to pay for the restoration of the oldest northern part, with its picturesque gable of timber and plaster.

Here a spacious bedroom once housed the maidser-

vants over the coachhouse, which was later turned into a kitchen. It was said to be haunted. A ghost rapped on the walls and trundled his own head about the fireplace. Unfortunately, the conversion, during which the huge fireplace had to be removed, appears to have upset the ghost. The Mellors saw no sign of him since they moved in.

The Mellor factory has since moved to larger premises near Hathersage. Broom Hall was sold to the Omega Group plc for use as its headquarters. It became part of the YMCA residential and leisure centre, which has now closed down. Part of it may become a nursery school in the future.

Whitley Hall

Elliott Lane, Grenoside

O
FF THE PENISTONE ROAD, sheltered in a hollow near the hamlet of Whitley, this old Hall has been a high-class restaurant since 1970 and a nine-bedroomed hotel since 1983 under the ownership of the Fearn family.

It was probably built in 1584, as on the stable is that date with *'William Parker made this worke'*. William Parker of Norton Lees leased it to Gilbert Dickenson, agent to the Earl of Shrewsbury, custodian of Mary, Queen of Scots, who is said to

have stayed there for one night in what is now a wood-panelled dining room.

It is of classical style and a palisade once ran across the front. A tunnel from a priest-hole leads to Ecclesfield Priory. It was once known as Loundside, Launder House or Lander House, from the adjacent waterhouse or lander house.

In 1616, it passed to the Shiercliffe family of Ecclesfield. A doorway in the added east wing bears the date 1683 and the initials of Dr Shiercliffe and his wife, Mary. By 1810 it was owned by Mr B. Hammond, of Liverpool, who soon afterwards sold it to William Bingley of Ellerslie Lodge, Penistone.

By 1812 John Rider was running a popular boarding-school at Whitley Hall for fifty to sixty boys, mainly from Sheffield. It lasted until the middle of the century. John Rider owned Greno House, and in 1852 George Rider, presumably his son, had a school there. Whitley Hall remained in the Bingley family until 1970. It was used as a hospital for American servicemen during World War Two.

The ghost is of a woman. A cleaning lady saw her in the toilets in 1977, and a man saw her around the same period in the Minstrels' Gallery. From her dress she was easily identifiable as Mary, Queen of Scots.

In 1994, a member of staff, Denise was scared by a shadow in the cellar. Betty, an elderly member of staff saw a ghostly 'lady in white' in the grounds.

Skew Hill Farm

Grenoside

....

ALSO KNOWN as Cross House, it was first recorded in 1601. The name may originate from the fact that it is situated at a crossroads, but it may also be because sometime between 1719 (the Toleration Act) and 1816 it was a school run by nuns.

In the nineteenth century, lighter trades such as file-cutting flourished in Grenoside because of the problems of transporting heavy materials uphill from Sheffield. From the 1930s, because of improved methods of production in the city, industry in Grenoside became almost extinct. The workshops of the little mesters were mostly demolished, and the quarries, such as the nearby Cross House Quarry run by A. Beever and Co, from which came stone to build the workshops, were closed.

Many farmers had done file-cutting in their spare time, and to this day the family at Cross House find files strewn about the yard. Three adjacent cottages have now been demolished.

In 1966, when Julie was four years old, she came downstairs and told her mother, 'That nice lady's in our bedroom.' She saw her four times within a month, waking up at night to see the lady sitting in front of the dressing-table. She would look at her through the mirror and then turn and smile at her.

Julie saw her frequently after that. When she was twelve she described her as a nun and very pretty. When Rita went into the room she felt a strange atmosphere as if something was rejecting her. When Julie was in her fifteenth year, she said that the nun had been in her bed to warm it for her.

As she grew older, Julie began to reject her, and one night came downstairs terrified because the nun had touched her on the cheek after warning her. Rita thought that the nun was saying goodbye. Now that Julie was grown-up, she no longer needed a protector. Or did she never appear again because she realised Julie was rejecting her?

When her brother John was four, their mother changed their bedding but forgot to put the sheets back onto the children's beds, so she told the children to sleep in their own double bed while their parents tried unsuccessfully to sleep in the smaller beds. Suddenly there came a sound as of breaking glass. The parents rushed into the bedroom, but the children were asleep and there was no sign of any broken glass.

Thundercliffe Grange

....

T O THE NORTH-EAST of Shiregreen, Thundercliffe Grange, at one time known as Effingham Manor, is built slightly to the east of the site of a twelfth-century hermitage. When the hermit grew old, the land passed to the monks of Kirkstead, Lincolnshire, who probably introduced the iron trade into the neighbourhood. Then called Thundercliffe or Synocliffe Grange, it was the residence of their bailiff who supervised their outlying lands and iron works.

At the Dissolution of the monasteries, it passed to the local gentleman Thomas Rokeby, and in the middle of the sixteenth century it was either re-modelled or rebuilt. In the latter part of the eighteenth century it was acquired by the third Earl of Effingham who demolished it and, using many of the original materials, built the present house in classical style in 1774.

The family stopped using the house in the 1860s and rented it out as a private residence up to 1916, when it became a private asylum for ladies. One woman was killed in the laundry copper. In 1930, it was acquired by Dr Mould, who ran the hospital and also lived the life of a Lord of the Manor.

In 1948, it was sold to the then new Health Service and became a home for mentally-ill and retarded children. It was closed in 1978 as being out of date, and stood empty until 1980 when a consortium of local people bought it for conversion into self-contained flats for twenty-six people, including children.

In its chequered history, Thundercliffe Grange, where Sir Walter Scott wrote *Ivanhoe* and Lord Byron was once a resident, has acquired a ghost.

It is said to be that of a woman in grey, who walks a certain corridor seeking her lost child. She is of a particularly repulsive appearance, with weeping sores plugged by tufts of hair. She is seen only at night.

Night staff of the children's hospital tried to operate a Ouija board in the corridor. It tipped over and broke. A student who was a part-time nurse slept there. The next morning he was missing and staff found him huddled in the corner of a small room nearby, demented. He had to be taken into hospital for treatment.

Bramley Hall
Bramley Hall Road, Handsworth
....

A LTHOUGH NOW surrounded by a housing estate, Bramley Hall is still a privately occupied family house. The present house is a fine example of eighteenth-century farm architecture, being built in 1710. A tunnel now blocked up connected it to the Manor House, and the pillars of the gate separating the garden from the old stables, now a separate house, originally came from Sheffield Castle.

The original hall on the site, however, was probably twelfth century. In 1190, there is a record existing of a grant by a Norman Lord, Robert de Lovetot to Richard de Acton of land at Bramley for a yearly rent of 5s-6d. This land was later granted by Richard de Acton to the monks of Kirkstead Abbey, Lincolnshire, who were very active in farming and mining around Sheffield. A grant dated between 1200 and 1218 by Hugh de Bramley gave the monks his land at Bramley except for one field which is now known as Dove Flatt, between the Hall and Myrtle Bank, which acted as a division between the Hall and the land given to the monks.

One day a monk of Kirkstead Abbey, on his way to Sheffield, was attacked by thieves who left him lying badly injured in a hedgerow near Bramley Hall. The following day servants from the Hall found him and carried him inside. His wounds were treated but he had lost too much blood and he died the day after.

According to legend, every year on the anniversary of his death, the monk returns to Bramley Hall to wander around the garden and rooms. However, he is friendly because of the kindness shown to him by Hugh de Bramley. He smiles benevolently at all who see him and raises his hand in benediction.

The owner of Bramley Hall since 1946 said in 1982 that she had not actually seen the monk, though his might be the grey shape that passes the french window at the back of the house. It is said that pools of blood appear on the path there.

Twice a year at one in the morning the lion-headed knocker on the side door raps very loudly, but there is never anyone there. The lady of the house had seen a black dog on the landing and often heard him sniffing.

Once at dusk she entered the lounge and saw a woman seated there, who at once got up, walked towards the french window and vanished. She wondered if it was her dead mother who had often visited the house, but could not be sure. Mr Briggs, an electrician, was working in the cellars – which date from Charles I's time – when he had the eerie feeling that someone was there with him.

Even the very architecture conspires to strike fear into the unwary. Approaching the stained-glass window at the front of the house upstairs, you receive the impression that something is coming out at you. Yet it is only a trick of the light.

Banner Cross Hall

Ecclesall Road South

....

SITUATED BETWEEN Brincliffe Edge Road and Carter Knowle Road is a magnificent Gothic mansion, which could be a perfect setting for one of Bram Stoker's tales of horror. Yet Lt. Col. Sir Francis Stephenson, who lived there just before the First World War, remembered it as a happy house. The present staff of Henry Boot, the railway contractors, who bought it by auction in the 1930s, don't admit to anything unusual.

The first house on the site was probably built in the reign of Henry VIII, when it

was known as Bannerfield after a nearby field.

It was called Banner Cross from the time of James I, from the salt cross which once stood at the southern end of Psalter Lane – said to be one of several crosses which marked the route taken by the salt traders across the moors from Cheshire to Sheffield, a trade in which at least one of the Banner Cross squires took part. The dark granite stone set into the main terrace is said to be the base of the cross.

A tapestry worked by Lady John Murray in the middle of the eighteenth century shows a plain Jacobean-style hall part of which was demolished in 1817.

From 1670 it was owned by the Bright family until 1748 when, through a granddaughter of the last of those to hold the Bright surname, it passed by marriage to Lord John Murray, a relative of the Duke of Atholl. Jeffrey Wyatt, a well-known architect who remodelled Windsor Castle, demolished and rebuilt the Hall for General Murray and his successor, the Reverend William Bagshawe. From the turn of this century until its sale it was leased to various families.

It seems to have been the old house which gave rise to the legend of ghosts. A poem published by Mrs Holland in the *Independent* in 1820 when the house was derelict says:

*. . . the mouldering mansion wears
In every view, the signal of decay,
Slow whispering winds creep through
the chilling rooms,
The tatter'd hangings shake with every breeze:
Through the long passages, and cold dark halls
(So fame reports) the flimsy spirits glide
In robes of white, or sweep the narrow stairs
In all the shapes of fear-formed misery.*

Yet, although no-one has admitted to seeing ghosts in it, the present Banner Cross Hall is associated with tragedy. Charles Peace, whose effigy can be seen in Madame Tussaud's Chamber of Horrors in London, is said to have played the violin to entertain the ladies at Banner Cross Hall.

He learned the skills of a burglar after being seriously injured in an accident at a city rolling mill. A master of disguise, he was a respectable citizen by day and a burglar by night. He took his 'skills' to many different towns. In and out of prison, he at last returned to Sheffield in August 1872 and settled in Darnall, where he fell in love with his neighbour's wife, Kathleen Dyson and pestered her despite a Peace Summons. When he went to Hull, the Dysons took the opportunity to move to Banner Cross. However, on his return, Peace tracked them down and shot Dyson through the head after firing at his wife, on November 29th 1876. Peace fled to London, where he was arrested after shooting a policeman. He flung himself from a moving train but in vain. He was hanged at Leeds on February 15th 1879, aged forty-six. He is said to haunt the *Banner Cross* pub.

The house where Arthur Dyson was shot is now 959 Ecclesall Road and is one of a terrace of renovated shops. Henry Boot are putting-up an additional building in the grounds.

Greystones Hall

Greystones Hall Road
....

ORIGINALLY the estates belonged to a branch of the Bright family. The old Hall was built in 1652 and was apparently still standing in 1885 when it was the home of Alderman Hunter's coachman, with the old smithy being used as a harness room. The present Hall was built around 1775 by Greaves of the firm of Greaves and Haslehurst, grocers, whose premises were on the site of Cole Brothers in Barker's Pool. When Alderman Hunter leased the Hall he greatly improved it and beautified the grounds. After various vicissitudes, in 1957 it became the offices of the Telephone Rentals Company.

The ghost of Greystones Hall is well-known in legend. A former owner, Sir John Pinkleton, had committed many licentious acts. His wife, Maria died aged thirty-two as a result of her unhappy marriage, leaving a son, William, and a daughter, Christine. William, like his mother, had a heart of gold and was loved by the peasants for miles around, who hated his father. Christine took after her father and as a result of her tale-bearing, he publicly horsewhipped William for fraternising with the peasants in the local tavern.

When William courted Virginia, the daughter of a local farmer, Christine told Sir John who, infuriated, thrashed William and told the farmer his daughter must go. The heir of Greystones could not marry the likes of her. However, the young couple eloped. They returned a year later with a month-old child to see Virginia's dying mother. Sir John was now a recluse, abandoned by daughter and servants and the Hall was badly neglected. He persuaded William to move in with his family and two servants. He became transformed. Before, he had extorted tithes; now the villagers praised his generosity.

He persuaded William to conduct some business for him overseas. When William left, Sir John insisted that Virginia occupy a first-floor bedroom on the north side, which Sir John had used when his wife was alive as it had a private staircase into the grounds.

The night after Virginia moved, on the 11th October 1871, she was found dead in bed, swollen and blackened. The livid hue of her lips aroused the servants' suspicions, but Sir John's physician said she had died of apoplexy over her husband's departure. She was buried in the grounds. The servants left, taking the child, and Sir John again became a recluse.

The villagers were frightened to see Virginia's ghost leave the Hall just after midnight, walk across the grounds to the farm where she was born, then return to the Hall and go up the private staircase to the room where she had died.

William returned to find his father feeble and deranged. He could not hire a servant because of the ghost. He visited the room at midnight and she suddenly stood before him, agonised fear on her face. She told him she had been murdered by his father on October 10th.

She was afraid when she walked abroad to seek her son. 'If I were loved, I could go peacefully on my way. People are afraid and run away from me.' She then asked him to kiss her. Overcoming his terror, he kissed her again and again. She vanished and a loud thud outside the door brought him to his senses. He opened the door and found his father lying there dead.

Virginia was avenged and never walked again through the grounds. But does she still linger in the Hall itself? Not so many years ago a caretaker saw a woman at the top of the stairs.

Since 1986, it has been the Greystones Hall Rest Home.

Greenhill Hall

Greenhill Main Road

························

SITUATED BETWEEN James Andrew Close and James Andrew Crescent, flats now occupy the site of Greenhill Hall, which was demolished in 1965. Only the stables remain, in use by the Public Works Department.

There is no documentary evidence as to when the house was built, but the style of the main door with its four-centred arch suggested a date around 1550. A stone in a secluded part of the garden bore the date 1667 and scratched on window panes were various names and dates, the oldest being John Lupton 1614.

A hall was standing on the site when in 1312 Sir Thomas of Chaworth granted to Beauchief Abbey his hamlets of Greenhill and Norton. It may have been this single, rectangular room, open to the rafters, which at the Dissolution of the Monastaries in 1536 went to Sir William West of the Inner Temple. He enlarged it with a thirty-foot kitchen on the north side and two bedrooms over the kitchen with access by a ladder.

In 1560, Jerome Blythe, of a well-known Norton family, purchased the Hall from Sir William West for his daughter Frances and her husband Thurston Kirke, of Whitehough Hall, Chapel-en-le-Frith. They inserted a second floor into the original building, so that it now had four bedrooms, kitchen, parlour and buttery. The eldest of the nine children, Gervase, was baptised in Norton Parish Church on April 16th, 1568.

Gervase, a wild youth, was disinherited. He became apprenticed to a London merchant in Dieppe, where he married and had seven children. He died in London in 1633, having returned in 1627. With others he started the Merchant Adventurers company to trade and fish on the 'south side of the River Canada'. He was granted a patent by Charles I to displace the French and found a colony in Canada.

Three ships were fitted out under command of his eldest son, David, with his brothers Thomas and Lewis. David helped to found the first British colony in Newfoundland, and Lewis with 150 men captured Quebec on the 27th July 1629, accepting the submission of the French governor Champlain and taking the French admiral Rougemont prisoner, together with the French war fleet, supply ships and a rich booty of furs. Returning to England, to the rejoicing of the English people and the fury of the French who burned effigies of the Kirkes on the Place de Grève, they discovered that peace had been declared and the conquered territory had to be returned to the French.

However, David and Lewis were knighted and David was made Governor of Newfoundland. After the defeat of Charles I, David was recalled by Cromwell. Both the Kirkes and the Bullocks, who followed them at Greenhill Hall, suffered for their loyalty to the Stuarts. In 1759, General Wolfe had the task of re-capturing Quebec.

The Bullocks, who had purchased half of Norton Hall estate from Anthony Babington, purchased Greenhill Hall in the 1590s, remaining there until the end of the seventeenth century. They enlarged it with the Oak Room on the south side and two upper rooms. The main staircase and the luxury of fireplaces were added.

John Lupton was the owner at the beginning of the nineteenth century for thirty years. He added three upper rooms and another long room with china and wine storerooms. The Listers followed the Luptons. In 1900, the farm was bought by Mr James Smith Andrew. During the Second World War RAF officers were quartered there.

In 1948, together with 197 acres of land, the house was bought for £31,000 by Sheffield Corporation, who were building a housing estate around it. The Hall with its gables and mullioned windows, was allowed to fall into disrepair and was demolished. The fireplace had an elaborately carved surround with the arms of the Bullock family in the centre. The ceiling and frieze were covered in fine plaster moulding, as was a similar ceiling in the bedroom above. The ceiling is now in Cartledge Hall, Holmsfield and the overmantel in Weston Park Museum.

The ghost of the Hall dated from the time of the Luptons. Once every five years at dusk a chaise was heard being driven furiously down the drive. Legend says that the girl's father had discovered the elopement. The young couple whipped up their horses, but on the curve of the driveway the chaise overturned and they were both killed.

The tenants during the 1950s always secured the shutters at dusk. On one occasion they were startled by a loud noise and discovered that all the shutters were flung open.

Burrowlee House

18 Burrowlee Road, Hillsborough

·······································

THE PRESENT ENTRANCE is at the back of the house on Broughton Road. Over the main doorway in the centre of the imposing Queen Anne facade is a date stone with *17 S 11* over *TE*. The present house was built in 1711 by Thomas Steade and his wife Elizabeth, probably on the foundations of an older cottage, which in 1539 was leased with five acres of land at Byrreylye (Burrowlee) in Olertongage (Owlerton) to Thomas Creswyke for 6d per annum. It was mentioned in the pre-nuptial agreement drawn up by Thomas Creswick and Henry Shawe in 1621 on the marriage of their children William Creswick and Anne Shawe. However, on the death of Thomas Creswick in 1640 the Burrowlee property was valued at only twelve shillings per annum. The Creswicks owned other properties but referred to themselves as yeomen, not gentlemen.

A later Thomas Creswick died in 1686, leaving two daughters. It was the younger one, Elizabeth who married Thomas Steade, a prosperous gentleman in 1696. In her husband's will of 1738 he left

Burrowlee House to her for her use during her lifetime. She eventually also inherited all the Creswick properties. A descendant, another Thomas Steade settled the house on his bride, Melisande Pegge in a marriage settlement of 1776.

The Steades later acquired Hillsborough Hall, now the public library, and rented out Burrowlee House.

In the 1860s, when the area of Burrowlee was not counted as part of Owlerton, the house was acquired by Samuel George Whitworth, a coal merchant, who married Anna Maria. It is Anna Maria who is said to haunt the house

Curiously, Anna Maria's great-grandaughter, who was born and grew up at the house in the nineteen-twenties, says that she was not aware of its being haunted then.

It was bought by Sheffield City Council, who used it as a school clinic from 1934 to 1984. It was then empty for a few years and the stonework deteriorated. The Hallamshire Historic Buildings Society persuaded the council to renovate it and it was used as a boys' club for a while.

It was again empty until it was bought by Mr Bryan Fisby, a high quality furniture maker and Mr Neil Trinder, a furniture conservationist. Sharing the house with a wood turner, woodcarver and designer, they have renovated furniture for stately homes such as Chatsworth, but also make new pieces. They renovated the house and grounds.

It was apparently the lady caretaker, when it was a boys' club, who first circulated the story of the ghost in order to deter burglars. Yet the ghost does exist. Part of the house, the cottage, was rented out. At first a girl lived on her own there and later her boyfriend moved in. They used to hear doors banging and other noises, when there was no-one else in the building. They were so terrified that they arranged for it to be exorcised. Mr Fisby's young son saw an old woman in a long, green dress on the stairs. A photo exists of Granny Whitworth, seated in the garden with her servants knitting for the soldiers in the First World War. A benevolent-looking soul, she is surely not to be feared.

Another legend is in the making. On the cottage side of the house in the back garden is a six-foot rectangular flower bed with perfectly straight sides, which flowers with a mass of bluebells in the spring. Does this grave-shaped bed conceal a horrible secret? Anna Maria's great-granddaughter says it was not there in her time and suggests it may be no more than the well-manured site of a cold frame.

It was known to have been a private residence in 1626 when it was occupied by the Parker family. Ann Parker, baptised at Norton in 1629, married Francis Barker, of Dore, whose family built Totley Hall. There were also family connections with the Pegges of Beauchief Hall. From 1747 it was owned by Thomas Ellin, the Master Cutler.

When Armitage wrote *Chantrey Land* in 1910 it was occupied by Mr W. Clarke. Armitage spoke of it as being haunted. The ghost is said to have been in one particular room, but the occupant in 1929, Mrs Thackeray, called the story 'rubbish'. It is not known if the farming family of Earps, the last occupants, experienced anything unusual.

Lees Hall

Norton Lees
....

SITUATED AT the northern end of Lees Hall Golf Course, Lees Hall was pulled down in 1960 as it would have cost too much to repair.

It was at least 350 years old, maybe even older than Beauchief Abbey. It, or a house on the same site, was said to have been occupied by monks from the abbey. A tunnel, now bricked up, ran from the cellar to the abbey. In the cellar was a massive hexagonal table around which the monks are said to have gathered. Another tradition makes it a place of refuge for Mary, Queen of Scots as she fled from her enemies. There is also said to be an underground tunnel to Manor Castle.

The walls were at least three feet thick and could have concealed secret panels and passages, though none were known by the twentieth century. It had a splendid oak staircase and oak panelling upstairs. In the old cart shed was a stone carved with *Pax* and *1732*. This is now displayed in the Lees Hall Golf Club house, which used to be Sheephills Farm until 1928.

Mosborough Hall Hotel

High Street, Mosborough
....

MOSBOROUGH HALL, now a picturesque hotel, is on the A616 between Sheffield and Chesterfield.

The name was originally Moresburgh, meaning 'fort on the moor' and it is mentioned in the Domesday Book. Parts of the present Hall date from the 14th century, although most of it was built in 1625, the façade being remodelled even later. The 14th-century section is at the rear and has

been restored as a cocktail bar. During the renovation five blocked-up tunnels were found, leading to Eckington Hall, six hundred yards away and to other buildings on the estate.

Among the more well-known owners of the Manors of Eckington and Mosborough was Sir William Dacre, whose son was involved in the plot to free Mary, Queen of Scots, when she was imprisoned in the area. His forces were defeated by Henry Carey. Lord Hunsden Carey was the son of William Carey and Mary Boleyn, sister of Ann Boleyn, and so the cousin of Elizabeth I. The grateful Queen gave him the Lordship of Eckington and Mosborough and made him a Knight of the Garter.

In 1660, the Manors reverted to Charles II and became separate. The Civil War had ended feudal tenure and Mosborough largely ceased to function as a manor.

The Stones family possessed the Hall from the middle of the 17th century until the late 18th century, when it was sold to a pharmacist from Rotherham, Pearson who modernised the building.

During the First World War men of the Nottingham and Derbyshire regiment were billeted at the Hall.

Private Peter Andrews slept in a bedroom which had not been used for many years. During the night he was aroused by the sound of a couple quarrelling in the lane below his window but could see nothing. The following evening he mentioned the happening in the *George and Dragon* nearby. A man called Joe told him he would see 'them' in the next night or two and he should move out of that room. He knew which room it was without being told. Bert Thacker, the landlord explained that it was haunted.

So that night Andrew's pals stayed with him playing cards, They all heard the voices more clearly. An anguished sobbing moved from a corner of the room towards the card table, then towards the window.

Gradually the room lightened near the source of the sobbing and they saw the apparition of an old bed upon which was seated a very pretty girl aged about twenty-two, sobbing. The soldiers fled.

Geordie, a local, told them how he was on fire-picket duty with a mate near the doorway to Hollow Lane, when they heard the voices and the words 'James' and 'Sir'. Geordie had no time to move before a girl ran through him into the Hall.

Dr Pilcher, their Medical Officer, said he didn't believe in ghosts and volunteered to sleep in the room. He slept uneasily. At 7am his batman went to wake him with a cup of tea. When Doctor Pilcher unlocked the door, the batman marched in and saw that the doctor's pillow and sheets were dripping blood onto the floor. The doctor had to be helped from the room, a whimpering wreck. He resigned as M.O.

In 1928, the occupants of the Hall took in paying guests. Mrs Grant, who lived in Hollow Lane, was then in her teens and helped with the laundry, in the old chapel, later the cocktail lounge. She went to hang up sheets in the drying room, when cold, clammy hands gripped her round the neck, though she could see no-one in the dim light. She managed to struggle free.

Her young brother went to the Hall to play with the tenant, Mr Hartley's son, who had a train set. Suddenly there was a rush of wind in the room, changing into a white vapour, which spun madly around. The walls shock and most of the pictures and mirrors fell from their hooks.

Their grandmother was baby-sitting at the Hall one evening. The boy was ill. She sat near the cot, sewing. Suddenly she saw a black dog in the doorway. It walked across the room to her and gently but firmly gripped her wrist in its mouth for a moment. It let go and then walked past the cot and out through the wall. The boy died the following day. Although the dog had not bitten her, its teeth-marks stayed on her wrist until her dying day.

She was seamstress at the Hall. Once, when it was being prepared for new owners, a schoolgirl friend called for her and they left together, locking the side door. The schoolgirl asked: 'Why have you locked that nice lady in the room?' Grandma then saw a beautiful young lady in pale grey looking out of the french window, then fading from sight.

The Spaffords brought in the local vicar, Montague Holmes, and Harry Price, the famous psychic researcher to exorcise the building, without success.

The Hall was derelict for 15 years before it was converted into a hotel in 1975 by Mr Nicholas. Both the Manor House and the Old Hall have been restored to their original grandeur with much of the original panelling and staircases retained. The principal bedrooms contain four-poster beds and these days are always the first to be booked up, particularly by foreign guests.

In early 1981 an American was conducted to the room assigned to him – number 9, also known as the Tudor Suite, a splendid room with a sixteenth-century four-poster bed and dark oak panelling. He halted at the threshold and said, staring apprehensively into the room: 'I'm not sleeping here. There's something here. You have a ghost, haven't you?'.

Yet until that moment, he had not known of the ghost of Mosborough Hall.

In 1692 a serving wench was made pregnant by the local squire, at least she accused him of being the father. In one version of the story she waited in an antechamber and when he entered his bedroom with his wife, confronted him. During the ensuing argument, he pulled out a knife and chased her out of the Hall and across the lane to the farmyard where he murdered her.

In another version she met him in the farmyard and threatened to blackmail him. Afraid that she would tell his wife, he pulled out a knife and chased her into the Hall, murdering her in what is now room

number 9, the Bridal Suite. Bloodstains on the floor were said to be irremovable, but were finally removed when the old floorboards were replaced during the hotel conversion. Even so, other guests besides the American have refused to sleep in the room because, even not knowing the story, they have felt 'strange vibrations'.

Sam Beecher, architect for the conversion, said that he had felt odd vibrations and unexplained noises and felt nervous if alone there at night. His dog would not go beyond the first floor when he visited the Hall. The night porter felt cold air blown past him.

Most sightings of the 'White Lady' are of a girl running from the farmyard, across Hollow Lane and through the six-foot thick stone wall of the hotel, at a point where there was once a door. She has never been seen running out of the hotel and has never been seen inside it, but when she is seen it is always around September 8th.

The nephew of a nearby pub landlord, Mr Alf Drury, was on a visit from Wales. On the Saturday night he offered to take the dog for a walk. He was a tough man in his twenties but he came back shaking, hair standing on end. He said that he had heard a couple arguing and as he walked on down the lane a girl ran out of the farmyard and through the wall of the hotel.

On 9th September 1978 at 10.20 pm, Bernard and Elsie Spense were walking in the lane, which was darker than usual as a street lamp was out. They had never heard of the ghost. Suddenly some youths appeared out of the darkness ahead. The couple stopped, afraid of being mugged. Their fear of a violent attack changed to uneasiness as they realised that the gang was led by a young woman in a white gown. They were moving forward in pairs and were all clad in white. Their footsteps could not be heard. The youths walked within three feet of them and disappeared as soon as they were past the couple. The Spenses then realised that the gate from which they had apparently appeared did not exist – the hedgerow was particularly thick at that point!

In another sighting the 'White Lady' is reported to have been leading four or five children in grey culottes. Perhaps the youths were heavenly emissaries or priests, but it would be fascinating to hear an explanation of where she collected four or five children!

She apparently also haunts the road past Eckington Hall. One night a couple were driving down the hill from the hotel, when a woman ran out in front of them. The man jammed on his brakes but was sure he had hit her. However, when they got out of the car, there was no-one to be seen. Puzzled, they drove on. Only in the morning light did they see a dent in the car bonnet! They later learned that other motorists had had a similar experience there.

In 1983 two local women saw a 'vision', a woman in white, swirling mist on The Brow, near Mosborough Hall Farm.

In October 2000, Brian Nicholas sold the Hall to Saxon Hotels Ltd.

Beauchief Hall

....

EDWARD PEGGE, High Sheriff of Derbyshire in 1664, built Beauchief Hall in 1671, mainly with stones taken from the nearby Abbey. He died in 1679 and was buried in the Abbey.

In 1784, Peter Pegge assumed the name of Burnell when he became one of the heirs of D'Arcy Burnell of Winkburn, Nottinghamshire. Members of the Pegge-Burnell family owned it until 1909, when it was rented to William Wilson, who bought it in 1922. It was later the home of A. Kingsford Wilson, the Master Cutler.

It then had several owners, one of whom was Frank Crawshaw, a former city councillor and donor of the Abbey to the city. He constructed a string of six pools in the course of the stream which is the boundary between the grounds of the Hall and Beauchief Golf Course. At one time a furnishing company used the Hall for offices.

In 1958, it was acquired by the De La Salle Boys College. It was leased to the Beauchief Independent Girls' Grammar School and later used by the De La Salle College Teachers and Staff Association.

In May 1981, forty members of De La Salle Old Boys Association stayed all night in various rooms and more recently a group of Sheffield Venture Scouts camped out in the Abbey grounds. All were unsuccessful in their hopes of seeing any ghosts.

People who used the Hall reported hearing a mysterious pianist in a top room later found to be empty. Lights switched on and off, doors opened and closed by themselves and the numerous strange bumps in the night were so nerve-racking that a man living in a flat there in 1978 left because he could stand it no longer. Sometimes after the members locked up at night, the lights switched on again by themselves. The worst place was the ladies' toilets where the doors opened and closed of their own accord.

The 'White Lady of Beauchief' who has been seen gliding around the grounds is said to be the ghost of a young woman who committed suicide in the 1920s when the Hall was a family home. She was apparently a fine pianist. About the same period a man shot himself in the gun-room. It is not known whether or not he is responsible for some of the weird goings-on.

Fishermen by the ponds near the Hall have also reported that a monk watches them from the bushes.

In 1982 the Hall was bought by the Boulding Group, who converted it into a country club. In 1986 it was sold to Mr Keith Vessey, who converted it into a fourteen-bedroom hotel with conference facilities. In 1987 it again changed hands and became a hotel restaurant.

In 1988 it was bought by James Wilkes plc, who converted it into offices for their headquarters. Staff moved in in June 1989.

In the *South Guardian* of 6th September 1984 Jack Roebuck recalled how one evening just over fifty years previously he had been walking with his sweetheart, Alice (now his wife) up Beauchief Drive. They had just passed the driveway leading to the Hall and turned off in the direction of Bradway, when a figure in white rose up at the side of them and then faded away.

Mrs Roebuck said, 'We saw her face for about a minute and she left us in a cold wonder.'

When the Hall was a hotel and the entrance hall was a sitting-room, a roomful of people saw the White Lady walk across the end of the room furthest from the front door.

On Saturday 1st December 1990 James Wilkes' staff were holding a birthday party for Christine Hirst. One man and his fiancée arrived white-faced and shaking. Outside it was about eight o'clock with a full moon. As they drove through the gate, the man suddenly slammed on the brakes, as he saw the White Lady among the trees. She was just a white form in a long, flowing dress, with no face or hands. Looking

back, he could see a light inside the gate. He couldn't understand why his fiancée couldn't see it. In fact she was more frightened than he was. The figure had been about five yards from the car.

Norton Hall
Norton Church Lane
....

E DMUND OFFLEY succeeded his father at Norton Hall aged eighteen in 1751. He had two sisters, Urith aged fourteen and Hannah Maria aged eleven. Mary died in infancy.

The Offleys were non-conformists. On his father's death, his guardians, John Rotherham of Dronfield and Godfrey Heathcote, a Chesterfield solicitor, sent Edmund to Scotland (as English universities were closed to dissenters). Accompanying him was an Anglican clergyman, Rev. James Reed, a socially uncouth man whom Edmund detested.

In Scotland, Edmund made the acquaintance of Rev. George Carr, a minister of the English Episcopal Congregation in Edinburgh. Carr offered Edmund lodgings in his own house and to oversee his studies. With the approval of the Duke of Argyll, Edmund left Reed. His guardians had to agree,despite their wish for him to leave Edinburgh for Aberdeen. He refused to do so and even dismissed his father's old servant, John Rhodes.

Edmund Offley came of age in February or March 1754, but died unexpectedly later the same year. There was an even greater sensation when it was discovered that he had made a will in favour of Carr and his wife, cutting out his sisters.

On the day Edmund died, the gardener back at Norton Hall met his master, who asked him how he was and how things were at the Hall. Edmund took out a key, let himself in through the outer door of the old tower and went up the stairs which led to the roof. Only when he did not come down again, did the gardener and his wife search for him. The whole neighbourhood became alarmed.

Four days later four Scotsmen in tartans and bonnets asked to see over the house. When they were refused, they told the inmates that Edmund Offley had died on the evening the gardener had seen him. Then they left after breaking some windows. On the night of the Scots' visit, it was said that blazing lights were seen on the top of the tower and the pale, ghastly figure of the dead man stretched out his hands, imploring assistance.

Neighbours Robert Newton of Norton House and John Girdler volunteered to go to Scotland. After meeting the funeral party on the way at Ferrybridge and asking them to remain at the inn until they returned from Edinburgh, they went on to meet Carr and his lawyer and got him to relinquish all claims under the will and accept £3,940 instead so that the sisters should not be left penniless. In the days before forensic experts it was impossible to prove that Offley had been poisoned, but people continued to suspect Carr and his wife. Offley was buried at Norton a month after his death.

Records of earlier Halls on the site go back 800 years. The present Hall was built in 1815 by Samuel Shore; Sir Francis Chantrey described it as a packing case with windows. Its simple lines are probably more to the modern taste. Florence Nightingale was a frequent visitor. Later owners included Charles Cammell, founder of Cammell, Laird, and Bernard Firth, son of Mark Firth the industrialist and philanthropist who was Master Cutler 1867-68. When Firth moved away in 1916, it became a voluntary hospital and later a forty-two bed annexe for Jessop's Hospital . It later became the Beechwood Private Clinic from November 1972.

The Hall itself is certainly haunted to this day. In the oak-panelled visitors' waiting-room, some nurses on night-duty were drinking tea, when a man appeared. At first they thought he was a patient as he was clothed in white – until he walked through the piano and the wall behind it! In the same room at midnight a bell started ringing.

A member of the office staff described how, soon after the Clinic first opened, it closed down for the holidays. On Christmas Eve 1973, she was alone in the reception room, there being no-one else in the building. There was not even a breath of wind. The fire-doors suddenly opened wide and she heard the sounds of a banquet, people talking and laughing and dishes clattering. Then the doors abruptly closed again and the sounds ceased. She was so unnerved that she felt she could stay there no longer and she phoned her husband to fetch her.

In March 1981 she was seated in her office, which with the office next door is thought to have been the Music Room. The door between the offices was open and for a moment she glimpsed a man standing there in the doorway. Thinking that it was an old man who helped around the Clinic, she said, 'I have no more letters for the post'. But he was gone. She got up to look for him and the lady in the next office told her that the old man had left an hour before. She then noticed a sweet smell of flowers in the air.

There had been only six deaths at the Clinic by 1982 since it opened. Two deaths were preceded by someone seeing the ghost of the man and smelling the sweet scent of flowers.

An assistant cook who worked at the Hall when it belonged to Jessop's Hospital remembers very clearly the day she saw a lady dressed in crinoline walking down the back stairs.

Beechwood Clinic closed down in 1991, and the Hall lay empty. The coach-house was converted in 1995 into nine luxury apartments, and in 1999 the house itself was also divided into apartments.

Fulwood

....

A TUNNEL ran from fifty feet down the well at the Gell Street Brewery, being approached by a ladder inside the well. Another entrance to it was from the cellar in a house above Glossop Road. It was said to run in line with the present road up to old Fulwood Church (built 1837).

There is a tale of a ghost in the Fulwood end of the tunnel, which was once seen chasing a ghostly carriage and pair past Fulwood Hall (built 1620), now the *Fulwood Inn*, owned by the Mansfield Brewery and opened in May 1999.

In 1964, a man and his teenage daughter were driving home from Fulwood to Dore one night, when they were forced to halt as a dark figure crossed the road exactly opposite to Fulwood Old Chapel. It did not pause or turn, just vanished. During the widening of Whiteley Lane (Chapel Lane) workmen cut through part of an old burial ground in use before the chapel was built in 1728. At least four bodies were reburied in the large filled-in quarry opposite the chapel. Were their slumbers disturbed?

At Christmas 1920 a party was held at Fulwood Head Farm. When Miss Nellie Humphreys wanted to return home to the *Sportsman Inn* on Redmires Road, Mr Digby Sutton gallantly escorted her and her dog. Returning to the farm just after midnight, he was suddenly seized with an ague, which he thought was another attack of malaria, from which he suffered. However, beside the violent shivering, he felt an inexplicable terror. His limbs were partly paralysed and he was sweating strongly. He managed to stagger on, and suddenly as he turned from Spencer Lane into Soughley Lane he became normal again.

Mr Silcock, his host, told him next day that there was a legend of a spectre at the junction of Spencer Lane and Soughley Lane which was so dreadful that no-one would go that way around after midnight.

One night at the *Three Merry Lads* inn, a farmer had wagered that he would ride down Soughley Lane from Spencer Lane at midnight. However, a hundred yards along Spencer Lane his grey mare halted, trembling with fright and suddenly bolted back into Soughley Lane.

Highlow Hall

Abney, near Hathersage
....

IF YOU TAKE THE A622 from Hathersage to Grindleford, and turn off on the right up a narrow hill road over bleak moorland to Abney, you will soon come to Highlow Hall, which stands back from the road on the left, a lonely stone-built outpost of civilisation, 800 feet above sea level. The Old English 'hlaw' meant 'hill', so its name means 'High Hill'.

It used to belong to the Eyre family, whose name Charlotte Brontë borrowed for the heroine of her novel. It is reputed to be the most haunted house in Derbyshire, with at least four ghosts.

Before the present house on the site there was a mansion, which was the chief seat of the influential Archer family. The last male Archer died in 1340, leaving two daughters as co-heiresses. Both were in love with Nicholas Eyre, a younger son of the Eyres of Hope. Nicholas dallied with both girls before finally deciding on the younger. The elder sister rushed from Highlow in a rage and killed herself. She is one of its ghosts. She laid a curse on the Eyres. All would go well with them for fifteen generations and they would acquire lands, knighthoods and marry into the highest families. Then they would lose it all, even down to the last acre.

She did not bother Nicholas, who was a tough character, with four sons, equally wild. The third son, Robert, had an especially bad reputation. He fell in love with Joan Bernake, daughter of the lord of the manor of Padley. Her father forbade the marriage, so Robert went off to the French Wars. He returned a hero, having been knighted in the field. A reformed character, he was allowed to marry Joan, with whom he had ten sons and four daughters, all buried in Hathersage Church.

Before his death in 1459 Robert built halls for his seven surviving sons. Some were new, some were existing farmhouses enlarged – Highlow was one. We do not know for certain which were the others – Moorseats, Nether Shatton, Hazleford, Offerton, Crookhill and North Lees are all candidates.

It was during building work at Highlow that Robert found some of the workmen playing dice during working hours. The short-tempered Robert ran a mason through with his sword, thus giving the Hall another ghost.

Robert also seems to have been responsible for a third ghost. He had gone to Chesterfield on business with a friend. Returning home drunk, they quarrelled and fought. The other man was killed. Robert survived because he was wearing a hard hat, which softened a blow to his head. A carving on the north wall of Hathersage Church is said to show him wearing this hard hat. According to legend he rebuilt the church as a penance for killing the mason.

The fourth ghost is another mason,

killed by a furious Nicholas, who overheard him 'chuntering' about his employer. This may be another version of the story about the mason killed by Robert.

The curse on the Eyres is probably a later story made up to account for the fall of the family, which was due to their clinging to Catholicism after the Reformation. In their heyday they were lords of twenty manors and owned more than 20,000 acres of land. Three Eyres daughters became countesses. As late as 1658 Robert Eyre of Highlow was High Sheriff of Derbyshire.

Mr and Mrs T. Wain bought Highlow from the Chatsworth Estate in 1950. They had lived there as tenants. Mr Wain's father had moved to Highlow when his previous farms had been drowned by the new Ladybower and Derwent dams. Another branch of the Wain family had been at Highlow since about 1900. A son and his wife turned the house into a restaurant, catering for functions such as wedding receptions, but it is still a private residence, not generally opened to the public.

Highlow, built of local gritstone with a local slate roof and massively thick walls, was probably once much larger than it is today. It is mainly 16th century with some parts older still. The older portion has small leaded windows, which are typically Tudor, the later wing has Georgian sash windows. A massive oak front door studded with iron leads through a porch into a long entrance passage with the more modern rooms, only three hundred years old, on the right. It is on the left-hand side, in the great banqueting hall with its huge open fireplace, oak-beamed ceiling and stone-flagged floor, dating back to 1550, reached by way of a splendid Jacobean staircase, that one might imagine the ghosts. Outside is a dove-cote and farm buildings and a water trough beside which was seen quite recently the ghost of a woman. A medium taking part in an ITV programme on ghosts, filmed there one Christmas, claimed to feel the presence of a male ghost. A woman visitor thought she saw a man's ghost.

In July 1996, the Hall was taken over by its new owners, Barrie and Penny Walker from Holmesfield, who were thrilled to recognise in Charlotte Brontë's description of the gate at Thornfield Hall their gate at Highlow. With grants from English Heritage, they embarked on a restoration programme, which included a new roof, uncovering the foundations of the part of the house which had been demolished. It used to be three times as large. Restoring woodwork and replacing windows it re-opened for Bed and Breakfast and – for a time – formal dinners in the Great Hall.

Renishaw Hall

Renishaw
....

BETWEEN THE VILLAGES OF Eckington and Renishaw on the A616, two miles from Junction 30 of the M1, the home of Sir Reresby and Lady Sitwell was built about 1625 by George Sitwell. The original house survives as the core of a much larger building, which was mainly the work of Sitwell about 1800. Some alterations had been made by Platt of Rotherham in 1777. The additions between 1793 and 1808 by Joseph Badger of Sheffield converted it from a small, compact house to a long, rambling and castellated one with Georgian windows. The library, formerly the Great Parlour, still has its original plaster ceiling with designs of lions' heads, squirrels, dolphins and mermaids. The stucco ceiling in the ballroom is attributed to Chantrey, who visited Renishaw with his master, Robert Ramsay. The impressive stables were designed in 1794 by Badger.

The best known inhabitants were probably the poet siblings, Dame Edith (1887-

1964), Sir Osbert (1892-1969) and Sir Sacheverell Sitwell (1897-1988).

The museum, art gallery in the stables and Italian gardens are open to the public on Friday, Saturday, Sunday and Bank Holidays between Easter and September and the Hall by special arrangement. Other attractions are the gallery café, craft workshops and gift shop.

In 1885 there was a party for Sir George Sitwell. The many guests included the Archbishop of Canterbury, Dr Tait, and his daughter. Miss Tait occupied a bedroom at the head of the stairs. In the middle of the night she was awoken by what felt like three cold kisses on her face. She fled to the room next door belonging to Sir George's sister and learned that she and other ladies had had similar experiences in that room.

Later architectural alterations included altering and enlarging the staircase. The haunted room and the one beneath it were abolished and incorporated into the staircase. Workmen uncovered an empty coffin fastened between the joists of the floor of the haunted room. The coffin was dated to the seventeenth century and was made with nails instead of screws. It was securely attached to the joists by iron clamps and because of the narrow space, it had no lid. It is not known whose coffin it was.

On September 17th 1909, Sir George Sitwell wrote to Lord Halifax that two ghosts had been seen the previous Saturday at the Hall. After dinner, Lady Ida was lying on a sofa in the upstairs drawing-room facing the open door. She saw in the passageway a servant woman aged between fifty and sixty, with grey hair in a bun under a white cap, a blue blouse and dark skirt. She moved very slowly with her arms outstretched at full length and hands clasped. She glided furtively, as if wanting to escape notice, straight towards the head of an old staircase, which had been removed twenty years previously, then disappeared. Everyone rushed out of the drawing-room but saw nothing.

They were returning to the drawing-room, when one lady saw in the full light of the archway below, twenty feet from where a doorway used to lead into the haunted room, the figure of a lady with dark hair and dark old-fashioned dress, apparently lost in thought. The figure was opaque and cast no shadow. She glided along and melted away near the walled up doorway.

Norton Grange

Bunting Nook

N ORTON GRANGE is a privately-owned house on the corner of Bunting Nook and Matthews Lane.

It was probably built in 1744 by Joseph Offley of Norton Hall for his chaplain. On the ceiling of the hall is the date 1744 and a repetition of the monogram *J.O.* After alterations in 1852, this date and a shield were inscribed on the mantlepiece in the dining room.

In the late 1960s, Mr A. Dewhurst-Smith restored the house as near as possible to its original state.

Joseph Offley died in 1751. His chaplain, the Reverend Daniel Lowe, ran a school at Norton. A later occupant of the Grange was the Reverend Henry Hunt Piper (1782-1860), a native of London. He began as a Congregationalist but later became a Unitarian. He founded a school at the Grange, 'Which promised well at times, but shrunk at others, and ultimately was closed'. Stones from the Unitarian chapel can still be seen, with a Corporation street sign fixed on them.

The school, which was detached from the dwelling-house, was at first for girls and none too successful. In 1814 it became a boys' school, charging 50 guineas, cheaper than many. By 1820, the school was flourishing, but by 1833 it was down to eight pupils and was closed. Some of the land attached to the house was used partly as a playground and was partly cultivated by Rev Piper, who had pupils from as far away as Edinburgh. A friend of James Montgomery, the poet, and Sir Francis Chantrey, the sculptor, Piper moved to London in 1843.

The house itself apparently has no ghost. Indeed, Mr and Mrs Holmes, who moved in in 1980, said that the house has a comfortable and welcoming atmosphere. However, being open-minded, they were very hopeful of spotting the horseman who

is reputed to jump over their garden wall into Bunting Nook.

Many years ago when the then mistress of the Grange was in labour, her husband,

in his hurry to fetch a doctor, jumped his horse over the wall by the summerhouse instead of going round by the gate. His horse fell and both were killed.

Incidentally, in all my researches, it was only on the front porch of Norton Grange that I experienced anything approaching a 'creepy' atmosphere. Perhaps an overactive imagination fed on tales of the boggards of Bunting Nook, combined with the complete absence of any other human being or even a bird on a still, sunny day, gave me an overwhelming urge to escape into Matthews Lane.

At that time I had not heard the story of the phantom horseman. Yet I am not alone in experiencing the eerie atmosphere of Bunting Nook. A certain young man, in 1985, visiting his girlfriend, turned into the lane from Hemsworth Road and was overcome with an oppressive feeling of a great sorrow. It was only as he reached the almshouses that the oppression was lifted.

He had a similar experience there on another occasion. He was so distressed that when he reached home, he broke down and cried.

Why do no birds sing in Bunting Nook?

Cliffe House
(Callywhite Function Centre)
Green Lane, Dronfield
....

BUILT IN 1760 at the junction of Green Lane, Mill Lane and Callywhite Lane, Cliffe House was owned by Samuel Jebb until 1785, when it was bought by Mr Michael Shaw. He was followed by the Rev. David Clarke, Minister at Dronfield Independent Chapel, fore-runner of the Lea Road Congregational Church, from 1813-19 and from 1829 to 1848. His widow, Mary, lived on there until her own death in 1867. Their daughter and her surgeon husband, Henry May, then took over until his death in 1887. In 1895 Dr Samuel Rooth and another surgeon, Arthur Dobson were at the Cliffe. Mrs Rooth lived on there from 1924 until 1933. Miss Charlotte Ward was the best-known owner, from 1944, having a local reputation as a tyrant. On her death the house was left to the Lilyman family, one of the brothers being a white witch.

Miss Ward lived alone. A niece visited her in term-time and on her last visit died mysteriously. Thereafter Miss Ward kept her bedroom locked up, leaving it exactly as it was when her niece died. When the house was bought by Surewheat Ltd, they had to break open the door and found dresses still hanging from the wardrobe doors and everything covered in dust and spiders' webs. Dresses and bed linen crumbled at a touch.

Chaplin's Wine Bar opened on the 17th June 1984. Peter Yates and his wife, the former Jill Saxby, Miss Yorkshire Television and Miss United Kingdom, kept the character of the house, which was decorated in stylish Victoriana. In the one-and-a-half acre garden there was a sixty-foot deep well, which became a wishing well.

The house had deteriorated and there were no modern conveniences. Now it was restored to something of its former glory, although some inner walls were knocked down. What did the little old lady in white think of it all as she stared smilingly out of the window at the bend in the staircases and saw a car park where trees used to be? She was not the only permanent resident.

Customers felt a presence in the gents' toilet upstairs, and sounds were heard from upstairs as of a man with a peg-leg moving across the floor. He is said to be a former patient who died and returned to haunt his doctor.

It later became the *Callywhite* Pub. By 1991 an extension was built. Planning permission was given for a house and garage in the grounds, but in 1994 developers, Cannon and Jones, asked for planning permission to demolish Cliffe House and build a supermarket amid great opposition from local conservationists.

It opened again in November as the Callywhite Function Centre for wedding receptions, functions and conferences, but Cliffe House was later demolished and replaced by a purpose-built residential nursing home, which opened in 1997.

The Hall
High Street, Dronfield
....

BUILT between 1700 and 1725 on farmland belonging to the Cecils. Despite alterations and modernisation, with its balustrade, symmetrical Queen Anne facades and centrally-positioned main door, The Hall still preserves a bygone elegance.

Some walls are four-and-a-half feet thick, accommodating wig cupboards. There is evidence of a previous Elizabethan house on the site.

For seventy years members of the Lucas family lived there. Helen and John Tym moved in on 4th July 1978. The family lived at the back while in front Mr Tym had his solicitor's office. In 1982, Mrs Tym converted the stable block into a nursery school.

The house and gardens are reputed to be haunted by a white lady, but the Tyms neither saw nor heard anything unusual. Indeed, the house has a friendly atmosphere. The Tyms moved out in 1988.

The Manor House

Dronfield

·······································

T THE BOTTOM of Wreakes Lane, the public library is housed in the old Manor House.

The manor of Dronfield is first mentioned in the record of its sale on 1st June 1567 *'with all appurtenances including coal mines, which he lately bought from George Barley, Esq.'* by Francis Rodes of Stavelay Wudthorpe, Esq. to George Selyoke of Hasilbarowe (co. Derby), gent.

In 1590 William Selyoke and Roger Gregory the elder of East Stockwith (Lincs.), gent, sold it to Anthony Blithe of Byrchet (Co. Derby). In 1645 it was sold by Charles Blyth the elder to George Holmes of Clowne, clerk, and Huntingdon Smythson of Boulsover, gent. Ralph Burton became Lord of the Manor in 1702 and he had built the present house by 1710.

A map showed the outhousing, gardens and two corn mills. In 1721 it was owned by Frances Burton, spinster and Mr and Mrs Clement Rossington. In 1746, Rossington sold it to John Rotheram, who married Elizabeth, daughter of John Fenton, who owned estates in Little Sheffield and Gleadless. Their daughter Elizabeth was unmarried. Before her death in 1797 she conveyed the Little Sheffield estates to Joseph Cecil and he also inherited Dronfield Manor.

Rotheram Cecil died aged twenty-four, leaving his widow with two young boys. At the outbreak of the First World War the boys, then in their early twenties, were called up. One was killed. The other came home, then went back to London and drowned himself.

Mrs Cecil lived on alone at the Manor until she died aged ninety-six.

The house was then sold in 1939 to Dr H. B. Fletcher, who presented it to Dronfield Urban District Council for use as council offices, with one small section for a public library. In 1967 the council moved to new offices nearby and the house was converted completely into a library. As the interior was worm-ridden, it was entirely gutted. Only the handsome wooden staircase is preserved, though removed to a private part of the building. Some of the original transomed and mullioned windows can be seen at the rear.

However, the building was re-roofed, which is unfortunate from a ghost-hunter's point of view. The old roof had windows in it and a grey lady used to look out at passers-by. One of the rooms upstairs, now gone, is said to have always been kept locked.

Since the renovations, the library staff have neither seen nor heard anything unusual.

Manor House Farm

Gosforth Lane, Dronfield

·······································

MANOR HOUSE FARMHOUSE and barn are Grade 2 listed buildings, but although the farm was recorded in the 1710 survey, there was no farmhouse until 1873, when Joseph Creswick was the occupier. Situated just behind the Manor House, it was always part of the Cecil estates and always tenanted till 1979 when Peter Cecil, who had inherited it from Mrs Rotheram Cecil, sold it to Barry Gwynn and his wife.

Mr and Mrs Gwynn spent a year renovating the house, and soon discovered that there was something unusual going on there. In the sitting room the Gwynns and their son and builders all heard a noise as if someone were running a stick over the fireplace.

In 1984 a decorator was at work in the sitting-room when he heard someone go upstairs and use the bathroom. Yet there was no-one else in the house!

One night when his parents were out, the son heard a crash as if a chimney stack had fallen. He phoned them up to tell them, yet when they arrived home, they could find nothing that could have caused the noise.

When they pulled down the shed at the south side of the house, they found hundreds of buried cat bones, the remains of the previous owner's pets. In the kitchen, out of the corner of one's eye, one frequently sees something flitting past at ankle level. Are the cats still there?

Manor Lodge

Manor Lane

••••••••••••••••••••••••••••

MANOR LODGE WAS built by George Talbot, fourth Earl of Shrewsbury, early in the reign of Henry VIII.

On Henry's orders, Cardinal Wolsely was kept at the Manor by the Earl for eighteen days when he was taken through Sheffield in 1530 on his way to face trial in London. A sick man, he did not survive the rigours of the journey.

From 1570 to 1584, George, the sixth Earl was custodian of Mary, Queen of Scots, who was confined either at Sheffield Castle, Manor Lodge or Chatsworth House.

Mary's health suffered during her imprisonment and to make her life easier the Earl had a turret or summer house built at the Manor for her, where she could occasionally take in the air on the flat roof and watch the hunting of deer.

In 1706, Manor Lodge was dismantled and its treasures removed. The house was allowed to fall into ruin. The eighth Duke of Nofolk preferred to live in the insignificant house in Norfolk Row, 'Lord's House' which he had built for his own and his agent's occasional use.

The Park was divided into farms and the rest of the trees felled. The great gale of 1793 blew down one of the two remaining towers of the Lodge and the local people carried off many of the stones.

Only the Turret House now remains complete, surrounded by large housing estates. It has been completely renovated and is open to the public in the summer.

The main interest for visitors is the quite small Queen Mary's Room with its stained glass windows, decorated plaster ceiling and the carved arms of Shrewsbury over the fireplace. There is a legend that it is haunted by a grey lady, identifiable as Mary, but the present caretaker has been in charge since 1967 without seeing anything unusual. It could be that the unhappy Queen, who arrived in Sheffield in her glorious prime and left it a wreck of an old woman, has flitted too.

Mrs Ida Elliott used to spend a lot of time with her husband's mother and old aunt, who lived at the Turret House. On the Sunday following the coronation of King George VI the aunt said that she had seen Mary Queen of Scots on the night after the coronation. The aunt had been sitting in bed drinking cocoa, when a beautiful woman in a long black dress glided across the room, evaporating into the opposite wall.

Mrs Ida Elliott was never allowed to stay the night. Other visitors, who had slept there, had felt as if they were being smothered and had to fight off their unseen assailant. People outside had seen someone dressed in a cape and cowl peering out through a window. The stone coffin outside, used as a horse trough must have retained the spirit of its former occupant (who was certainly not Queen Mary), because the family dog avoided it.

Queen's Tower

Park Grange Road
·····························

A LISTED BUILDING, Queen's Tower was built in 1839 as an exact replica of Alton Towers, the twelfth century castle, now in ruins, near Ashbourne in Derbyshire. The builder, Samuel Roberts, was so interested in local history that he included in its structure a portion of the wall and a mullioned window from Manor Lodge.

Queen Mary is said to have looked through the window and scratched it with a diamond.

In 1973, a women waiting for a bus in Park Grange Road saw a cloaked figure glide across the road in the direction of Queen's Tower.

Mrs Lily Panting, who worked there as an office cleaner in the late thirties and early forties, was scrubbing the entrance hall when she saw a woman gliding towards her. She paused at the bottom of the stairs, then floated up the stairs and disappeared. Mrs Panting did not see her face. She saw only that the woman was wearing white stockings, white bloomers and black buckled shoes. Mrs Panting went straight into the stores and the storekeeper said, 'You look like you have just seen a ghost'. She replied, 'I might well have done.'

The sports firm Ballarat Ltd bought it in 1976 and have turned the former walled garden into a squash club. There are plans to turn the house itself into a hotel and to have a disco and restaurant in the stables and a casino in the cellars. At present one of the directors and his family have a flat upstairs in the house.

In August 1980, Mrs Sue Oades was sitting in the car with the lights on, while her husband went back into Queen's Tower for something he had forgotten, when she saw a figure in the porch way. It was the top half of a man fading away below. He crossed from one side of the porch to the other and vanished.

During the summer of 1981 she was in the lounge when something touched her on the shoulder and extreme cold whirled around her. The curtains moved and there was a sweet, cloying smell so strong that she felt overwhelmed and off balance. Then suddenly the cold and the smell were gone. However, she felt no fear. The same thing happened on another occasion, though the smell then was not as strong.

Mrs Oades, however, says that she is sure that the house is friendly and she would not mind being there alone at night. The building has many secret panels. Some years ago, during a children's party, something in a grey dress floated through a wall. Children and adults ran outside screaming.

WOULD-BE ghost hunters should be aware of seeing ghosts in every unusual phenomenon. As one lady put it, 'We have three poltergeists in our house – the kids!' It is only when every other explanation fails to account for mysterious noises, gliding figures and objects moving apparently of their own accord that one should think of the supernatural.

A police-sergeant described how easy it was to let your imagination run away with you as you patrol the streets at night, especially when you are feeling tired. Shadows take on menacing shapes. Patches of mist suddenly form and are as suddenly dispersed leaving you wondering if that was a human shape or not. It is only when other people have seen the same thing at the same spot, that you can allow yourself to think, 'Maybe it was . . .' Even so, doubters would cite mass hallucination as an explanation.

Any old, derelict house or the scene of a tragedy is liable to gain the reputation of being haunted, but all too often one would be hard pressed to find someone who has actually seen anything out of the ordinary and not merely been scared by their imagination.

A house, now demolished, in Pearl Street off Cemetery Road, Sharrow, also had a reputation for being haunted. Every night at the same time mysterious knockings were heard and the house began to shake. People congregated to hear it, although others were afraid to pass it on their own at night. On December 7th 1881, such was the mass hysteria that one spectator dropped down dead of a heart attack. Subsequent investigations, however, discovered mine workings directly under the house.

People flocked to see a 'ghost' in Chapel Walk in the city centre, until someone realised that it could only be seen from a certain angle because it was caused by the reflection from a particular street lamp.

Some 'ghosts', however, have proved to

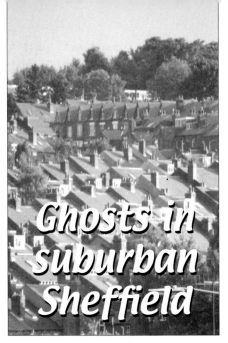

Ghosts in suburban Sheffield

. . . but first, a Word of Warning!

be deliberate hoaxes. In 1843, when Sheffield's largest private bank, Parker, Shore and Company, in Bank Street, was forced to close its doors, Dorothy Shearwood lost the money she had inherited. For some years she nursed a grievance against certain Sheffield businessmen whom she felt were to blame. Then one night they were going up Toad Walk near the General Cemetery at Sharrow, where James Montgomery, the journalist and hymn-writer (1771-1854), is buried. She sprang out at them dressed in a nightdress and a tasselled nightcap such as Montgomery used to wear. The men were so terrified, they vowed to build a church as restitution for their unkindness to Montgomery when he lived at The Mount on Glossop Road. The church they built is said to be St. Stephen's in Fawcett Street, off St. Philip's Road. Dorothy Shearwood made several appearances as the 'ghost' and the people round about became so scared that a huge policeman with a blunderbuss was sent out. He shot her nightcap off. Needless to say, the 'ghost' never walked again.

The most famous fake to fool a credulous generation, however, was 'Spring-heeled Jack'. He first appeared about the year 1800 and was also known as the 'Park Ghost'. He was said to spring like a goat and jump through walls and five-barred gates. Dressed in white robes he appeared at all times of night, suddenly jumping out in front of people, mostly courting couples, and just as suddenly vanishing when anyone tried to grab him. He came out from what were later the grounds of the Cholera Monument near Norfolk Park and also terrified citizens at Skye Edge and Arbourthorne.

People took to carrying sticks at night and going out in crowds. Things soon became too hot for the 'ghost' and he ceased his 'haunting'. He was, it was hinted, a member of a well-known family from the Park district, noted for his twisted sense of humour.

Nearer our own time, in 1934, Froggatt Edge, already noted for the Roman soldiers who are said to march in never-ending line across the track leading from Owler Bar, acquired a 'White Lady'.

She was seen on dark nights flitting among the rocks overlooking the valley towards Grindleford. The gamekeepers for the Duke of Rutland heard that a woman-like form crossed the moors without leaving footprints in the snow, but were canny enough to suspect it was a trick dreamed up by poachers after game for the Christmas market. The keepers spent the cold night watching the moorlands and spied a figure moving towards Baslow village carrying something resembling a pheasant. Yet no tracks were to be seen. However, there was a remarkable absence of birds and rabbits from that stretch of moorland. The keepers knew they had been tricked, but only years later did they discover how. The son of one of the poachers disclosed how his father had had his most profitable Christmas that year. A woman's old nightgown and a stuffed pheasant were pulled along a wire strung between trees near the road in order to keep the police and gamekeepers there while the poachers were clearing game off Froggatt Edge to be sold in Sheffield. The men working the wire had plenty of time to remove it before joining the keepers and villagers in the hunt for the 'ghost'.

But the best story is from Attercliffe. In the days when snatching bodies for sale to medical schools was a profitable business, until the notorious case of the murderers Burke and Hare in Edinburgh made the schools think twice about buying bodies, a soldier was making his way from Rotherham to Sheffield.

It was about dawn when he spotted a cart on Attercliffe Common near the graveyard and wearily climbed in, hoping for a lift or at least a rest. Suddenly, a body was bundled in, two men followed and drove off.

On the uneven ground the soldier was jolted against the legs of one of the men, who pushed him back, exclaiming, 'By gum, it's warm.'

The soldier stretched forward his red-coated arm and said in sepulchral tones, 'Aye, and if tha'd cum fra wheer awve cum, tha'd be warm.'

The men fled, terror-stricken and the soldier triumphantly drove the cart to the police-station to collect his reward.

High Green

Charlton Brook Estate
....

I N DECEMBER 1994, Sue and her student daughter told how they would wake up at 6 am in their house on Pembroke Crescent to hear what sounded like a foot-

ball being kicked around the attic. They were quite used to it after nearly three years. 'We shout out for it to shut up and it usually does.'

In 1993, Sue sometimes saw an extremely thin man in Victorian dress. Then as she stopped seeing him, her daughter started seeing him. One night they each drew a sketch of him and proved that they were seeing the same man in black.

There had also been a lot of banging in the daughter's room and things were inexplicably found broken. They were getting so fed up that they were thinking of trying to have the house exorcised.

Stocksbridge By-Pass

....

THE BIGGEST STORY of recent years concerns the A616 Stocksbridge by-pass, which was built to divert heavy lorries from the centre of Stocksbridge. Seven miles long, it runs from Underbank to meet the M1. Costing £18 million, it was supposed to be a dual carriageway, but most of the road is two lane and part three-lane with a speed limit of forty miles an hour.

When it opened in 1988, responsibility for it passed from the Department of Transport to Sheffield City Council. A

heavy responsibilty, as it turned out, for some unknown official had decided to flout superstition and arrange for it to be officially opened on Friday May 13th!

Ever since there has been an unusually high number of accidents, many fatal. Driver error, poor road design and inadequate or non-existent lighting over some stretches at night have all been blamed. The Department of Transport eventually agreed to install lighting the full length of the road. The large black shadow that sat in the passenger seat of psychic June Beevers' Metro car in the spring of 1993 was undeterred by street lights.

'It didn't communicate with me,' she said, 'but I felt a real sense of fear. I was shocked and I am used to psychic phenomena, so it would be very startling for other drivers and I dread to think what the consequences could be.' She believes that this very active presence is responsible for the accidents.

There is one legend which says that a hooded figure, which has been seen by many people particularly around Pearoyd Bridge, is of a runaway monk (disillusioned with monastic life) who died at either Hunshelf or Underbank Hall. He wished to be buried at Stannington, but instead was buried in unhallowed ground far from his monastery, and his grave has been disturbed by the building of the by-pass. One man, who lives nearby, regularly sees the monk on the bridge. A man and a boy have also been seen on the bridge.

It is probable that his was not the only grave to be disturbed, although Stocksbridge vicar Reverend Brindley could find no record of a Christian graveyard in the area.

At seven o'clock on the morning of

September 8th 1987 two security guards, employed on the part-built road, arrived at the vicarage asking him to exorcise the road. One of them burst into tears and was in a state of shock.

The vicar did not know what to do and contacted the police. The guards, David Brookes and David Goldthorpe had been driving in a Landrover along the by-pass about midnight, when they saw a hooded figure on the bridge (which could not be reached on foot). They stopped and directed their headlights onto the bridge. The lights passed straight through the figure, which immediately vanished.

Shortly before this they had seen a group of children playing just down the road from the bridge near a pylon. They drove past, parked the Landrover and got out, but the children had vanished. There was fresh mud around the pylon, but no footprints.

John Holmes, who worked at G.R. Steynes' lorry depot on Carr Road, Deepcar, said that he and his mates used to hear children singing while the construction work was going on. Even on freezing nights, they heard what sounded like a choir of about ten children, but could never make out the words. They always felt that they were being watched. One old man refused to work at the depot at nights, because he had seen something there.

At midnight on September 12th, PC Dick Ellis and a special constable, determined to investigate the story, parked near Pearoyd Bridge. It was a clear night with an almost full moon.

After a couple of minutes they both saw a shadow moving across a large painted pallet. It happened three times. They decided that lights from the steelworks below were causing it.

Then suddenly PC Ellis froze. He felt that someone was standing beside him. He turned but could see no-one. Then his colleague let out a scream and hit him on the arm. He looked the other way and could see the torso of someone standing next to the passenger seat. He gained the impression of a Victorian cravat and waistcoat. For a split second he saw a face. Then the man was gone.

They drove up to the bridge and radioed to colleagues in Deepcar to join them. They had only been parked for a few seconds, when something thumped on the back of the car. Yet there was nothing to be seen. They hurriedly drove back down to the works.

In the autumn of 1987, Graham Brooke was training for the London Marathon and running with his son for company. They were coming down the road from Wortley Church, when they saw a man dressed in eighteenth century clothes with a dark brown cape and carrying a bag with a chain. There was a musty smell. As their hair stood on end, the man suddenly vanished.

In another report two women driving along the by-pass saw a man floating in mid-air.

In 1990, Melbourne Heptinstall was working as a night driver for Ernest Thorpe. He had pulled into the trailer park at Station Road, Deepcar and was taking the ropes off the back of the trailer, when he suddenly went cold. There was a musty smell and he saw the figure of a monk gliding through the beam of the headlight. Peter Thorpe said that other drivers had also seen it.

On New Year's Eve in 1997, Mr and Mrs Ford were driving along the by-pass into Stocksbridge when they saw a man apparently trying to cross the road. He wore a cloak, yet seemed to be hovering in mid air. As Mr Ford slammed on the brakes to avoid him, he froze with fear. the apparition had no face! His wife grabbed the wheel to prevent them from plunging over a steep embankment above the steelworks.

Stories of the hauntings go back to the beginning of the century. Only since building of the by-pass have they become more frequent or received more publicity.

There is a legend of a stage-coach overturning and killing a group of small children. Or were the ghostly children really fairy folk?

Another story concerns Berton-under-Edge farm, close to Pearoyd Bridge, where mysterious tapping noises were said to have been heard in the beerhouse into which a former weaving shed had been converted. Folk blamed the ghost of Nancy, who drowned in a vat of dye in the early 1800s.

Attercliffe Common

G RIM, THE MOST dreaded of all the Saxon gods, gives his name to Grimesthorpe, meaning 'Devil's village'. It is situated on the Don exactly opposite to Attercliffe, dedicated by the Romans to the goddess of revenge. It is not therefore surprising that this part of the Don was feared as the resort of demons and elves.

Attercliffe Common was enclosed in 1811. On fifty acres of common land and two hundred and thirty acres of wasteland there were once only three houses and a few huts. Down to recent times and the building of the factories and workers' houses, it retained its atmosphere of evil. Its wild landscape was a magnet for highwaymen.

Spence Broughton was the son of a prosperous farmer from Sleaford, Lincolnshire. When he was twenty years old he married a girl with a dowry of £1,500, which he squandered in riotous living. At last, desperate for money, he joined with John Oxley to waylay the post-boy George Leasley on the 9th February, 1791. He was caught and hanged on 3rd April 1792 at York.

The site of the gibbet where his body was displayed was in the yard of the Yellow Lion in Clifton Street, near Carbrook Hall. Part of the principal post of the gibbet was built into Orgreave Colliery, after it was taken down on 23rd September 1827. Spence Broughton has apparently returned to near the spot where his body was hung in chains on a gibbet at the site of his crime for thirty-five years, until only pieces of bone were left. These were turned into souvenirs such as ale-mug handles by the sensation-seekers who flocked to see him. His right hand is on display at the *Noose & Gibbet* formerly *The Stadium*, 97 Broughton Lane.

At Richard Wragg's, the builders' merchants, who were at 25 Broughton Lane from 1927 until 1998, a shadowy figure was seen in the cellar and yard, in one corner of which was the site of the gibbet. One of the tilers first saw it in 1980 and it was seen again in either April or May 1985 by the roofing manager, Brian Sheldon, who said, 'I saw what I thought was a customer standing by a cement mixer. Seconds later I turned round to serve him, but he had disappeared. I checked the yard and the street, but there was no-one to be seen. It looked like a person in a long, dark coat, thinking about it, it could have been a cloak.' Another employee saw it on a different occasion.

There was said to be a tunnel from Wragg's to Carbrook Hall, which is also haunted, but the entrance is now lost.

Loxley Common

·····································

JOHN OXLEY, SPENCE Broughton's accomplice, wandered the neighbourhood for weeks, hunted by the law. He went to see Broughton's body on the gibbet. Finally at the end of January, 1793 he was found dead of cold and hunger on Loxley Common.

On Loxley Common he must have seen the gibbet of Frank Fern, who in 1783 robbed and murdered a jeweller, Nathan Andrews who was passing over the common. He was captured the following evening, tried and executed. His body was then hung in chains on a gibbet near the scene of the crime. The skeleton only fell from the chains on Christmas Day, 1797. The gibbet post remained until after 1810. It is said that to this day anyone hardy enough to cross the Common at midnight will hear above the howling of the wind, the clanking of the gibbet.chains.

On New Year's Eve 1812, a woman acquaintance from the nearby hamlet of Wadsley came to a lonely cottage on the moorland to wish the compliments of the season to Mary Revill, wife of Lomas Revill, gamekeeper to the Lord of the Manor. In the early morning light she found Mary lying on the floor in a pool of blood, her baby asleep in its cradle.

Footprints in the snow led from the cottage to Loxley cave, but no footprints came out. Revill, found in his cabin in the woods, heard the news with little emotion. He had been drinking heavily at the village inn early the previous evening, but there was no proof that he had not slept at the cabin. For years afterwards he was said to act strangely on a New Year's Eve and he aged prematurely, with his hair turning white. He said he could not stand living. One New Year's Eve, when he had not been seen for some days, some men from the village went to look for him and found him hanging from a rafter in an outbuilding near the cottage. Later they found in the cabin a hunter's knife, rusted with blood, and blood-stained gaiters.

Mary's ghost is said to wander over the common when the snow is on the ground. Two girl riders may have seen her in January 1985. A young girl in a long dress ran across the snowy ground in front of them and vanished. Their horses were terrified and still showed evidence of their terror when they and their riders eventually returned to the anxiously waiting stable owner.

Wadsley Common

·····································

IN 1920 the *Independent* reported how on Wadsley Common – wild, hilly and overgrown with bracken, heather and a few trees – a woman in white walked between the hours of nine and eleven at night, raising her arms in lament and occasionally moaning. She haunted the neighbourhood of the Worrall to Loxley Road, near an old mine. She was seen by a farm labourer, Clarence Swain and his sister, a nurse, who were walking from

Hillsborough. Apparently she glided over a wall near the mine. She was also seen by a miner, John Grayson, who lived in a nearby cottage.

Some believe that the White Lady is merely the release of natural energy from the earth or the release and ignition of methane gas, a will o' the wisp.

Parson Cross

·······························

N DECEMBER 1994, Mrs Peacock wrote to *The Star* about her experiences in two houses in the Parson Cross area.

In 1947, her family moved into a brand new house on Colley Road. They lived there for nine years during which they saw 'things moving', heard noises and 'loud, evil mocking laughter'. Even her two-year-old brother saw 'a lady coming down't bannisters'.

In 1976 they moved to Wheata Road. This house became known for being haunted, so they had difficulty getting an exchange in 1991. 'Just some incidents, a rumbling, shaking staircase, heavy footsteps in the hall. An entity, complete with chains, coming out of the back bedroom and across the landing. This was witnessed by our visitors, not just family.'

Wordsworth Avenue

·······································

N DECEMBER 1994 a family fled their Wordsworth Avenue council home, unable to stand the strain any longer after living with ghosts for six years.

Doors opened by themselves, and the mother experienced sensations of some-

thing touching her around the hair. Her daughters, aged five and seven told of shadows following them and 'something with big ears.' The youngest daughter used to have screaming fits.

It was always cold, especially on the stairs, even with the heating on. In November the mother bought an old ottoman linen chest and things got worse. When the television came on by itself after the fuse had been removed, they had had enough.

Psychic researcher David Aldous investigated. While he was alone in the house, the toilet flushed by itself. He set up monitoring equipment. Infra-red video footage showed the most unusual and puzzling sight he had ever seen – strange bubbles of light that crossed the screen for a split second. He had no idea what he was dealing with and did not rule out an exorcism.

The council said that they could not let out the house to anyone else until the problem – which they put in the same classification as dry rot or rats – had been solved.

Busk Meadow Flats

Longley Estate
···

HEN STEVE RODGERS was fifteen years old, he used to baby-sit for his sister and her husband in their maisonette.

One night the baby had slept since about ten o'clock. At half-past-twelve Steve heard voices in the bedroom, yet there was no-one there but the baby.

Back in the sitting room he felt someone touching him on the shoulder and heard a young woman's voice whispering to him, although he could not make out what she was saying. This lasted for just a few seconds. When his sister and her husband returned, he told them about the voices. They said that they too had heard them. The baby had just started talking and was in fact talking to a ghost. The ghost entered the room through the ceiling, which the child regarded as quite normal behaviour, describing it as 'Not little girl, not lady.'

The ghost, who played with the child's toys, was Steve's sister's best friend at school. She had been killed in a motorbike accident aged fifteen.

They arranged for an exorcism, but she came back again. She was watching over the baby. Finally, in desperation, they moved house.

Wincobank

Merton Lane

ONE DAY IN 1932 it was dusk as Mr Ernest Commander sat on a wall in Merton Lane near the Wincobank Hotel with two young friends and his aunt, when an apparition like a cloud floated just above the ground along the opposite side of the road from where they were sitting. They watched, amazed and terrified as it disappeared past Gatenby's bakery, floating in the direction of *Wincobank Picture Palace*.

At about the same time a young girl, Jettie Smallwood, who lived in Prestwick Street, saw the ghost float slowly down the passage leading to the back door of her home and disappear into the outside toilet.

People organised themselves into groups to hunt it down. It is said to have finally been exorcised in Kimberworth Cemetery. According to one eye-witness: 'It caused no end of a stir at the time.'

Brightside

Upwell Street, Sheffield 4

IN A LETTER TO *The Star* of May 1st 1987 Mr K.L. Smith of Sheffield 12 described how, on December 15th 1940 during the Sheffield Blitz, when he was two years old, he and his mother were visiting his uncle's house in Upwell Street, when the sirens wailed.

He and his mother, his aunt and three-year-old cousin took shelter in the pantry under the stairs.

In the pantry with them the child saw a little old lady wearing a long dark dress, which he later learned was of a style worn at the turn of the century. She also wore a black poke bonnet and gold-rimmed spectacles.

As his mother held him, he looked over her shoulder straight into the old lady's eyes. Her face was expressionless. Then at the noise of a nearby explosion he buried his face in his mother's shoulder. When he looked up again, the old lady had gone. Later, when he described the old lady to his mother, she put it down to his child's imagination. He almost came to believe this himself.

Years later, in 1960, his cousin asked him one day, 'Who was that little old lady in the pantry during the Blitz?'

His description of the stranger tallied exactly with his cousin's.

Hillsborough Park

HILLSBOROUGH PARK was created on about 50 acres of land, bought, together with Hillsborough Hall, by the council for £15,000. The old Hall is now the public library. The park was officially opened on August 8th 1892 with four bowling greens, eight tennis courts and an up-to-date running track.

On June 20th 1994, Tina Greig and a woman friend were walking her Rottweiler in the park about one o'clock in the morning, when in the pitch darkness they saw what appeared to be a white top moving towards them very fast. They realised it was a woman cyclist in a nurse's uniform with a white blouse but they could not see her face. As she got close to them, she suddenly vanished. Even the dog froze with fear and they could not escape from the park fast enough.

The park-keeper, Gary Ainley, later told Tina that other people over the years had seen the cyclist, although he himself, who lived in the old park lodge, which was built in 1800, had never seen her.

In a letter to *The Star*, 'PG' claimed the ghost to be Miss Sanderson, a teacher at Malin Bridge School from 1910 to 1912. A keen cyclist, she has also been seen in Beeley Woods and along the lane near Wardsend Cemetry. She had also been seen by the writer's mother and two aunts. Are there *two* cycling ghosts?

took over in 1960, Sunday opening became permanent, until the cinema closed on 29th October 1967.

It was subsequently a bingo hall and then a succession of supermarkets. The great balcony is still there above the supermarket ceiling, together with the remains of the screen. The cinema ghost, known as Fred, is said to have thrown himself from the balcony when his girlfriend left him.

Hillsborough

Taplin Road

Hillsborough Park Cinema (now Netto)

Middlewood Road

AT THE CORNER WITH Catch Bar Lane, this cinema was designed by P.A. Hinchcliffe and opened on 10th February 1921. The proprietors were Sheffield Suburban Cinemas Ltd.

At balcony level there was a lounge, which for some years was used for whist drives. Attempts were made to establish it as a dancing venue. When Star Cinemas

IN A LETTER TO THE Star J.H. of Sheffield 6 told how, when he was a policeman stationed at Hammerton Road Station in the winter of 1967, he was on foot patrol near Hillsborough Corner. It started to snow, soon becoming a blizzard. He took shelter in a shop doorway. By 2.30 am the snow was four inches deep.

Suddenly a large dog, which seemed to be a cross between a greyhoud and an Irish wolfhound ran past him along Middlewood Road and out of sight into Taplin Road.

It seemed unusual, so he followed its tracks in the snow. There was no sign of the animal in Taplin Road, but the tracks led him up to a point near the Taplin Road garage, where they began to cross the road. Then in the middle of the road the tracks ended abruptly. The dog was still nowhere to be seen.

He never found an explanation.

The Arena

Broughton Lane, Attercliffe

....

THE ARENA WAS built for the World Student Games, which took place in July 1991. It was officially opened on 30th May 1991 by Her Majesty the Queen.

There is permanent seating on three sides yielding a capacity of 12,000 with the eastern end taken up by a 50,000 square foot exhibition area.

There is a permanent ice floor for ice shows and ice hockey, seating 8,000 spectators. There are four large team dressing-rooms for twenty-two people, which are sub-divisible, training areas and also four luxury 'star' dressing rooms. To accomodate the press there are two thirty-seat press boxes, a television interview room and two hospitality areas each over a thousand square feet. There is a first aid centre and a competitors medical centre.

The site was once covered by storage depots, a scrap yard and part of a public park, running alongside the Sheffield and Tinsley Canal. Three abandoned mine shafts were found on the site and 4,000 tons of coal was taken out to feed a nearby power station before the Arena was built.

In the eighteenth century, however, it was wild heathland. There are various claims for the site of the gibbet where Spence Broughton's body was displayed from 1791. Could it have been where Entrance 'C' is now situated?

Amanda Howe, a security guard at the Arena from April 1993 was on duty near the lift at Entrance 'C' at 9.30 pm on November 27th 1993 when she saw a dark figure of a man, about six-feet tall in the shadowy corner by the lift. The usual lift operator is about five-feet tall, so it was not he. The man vanished even as she looked. It is always cold near that lift and many people have remarked how eerie the Arena is at night. Could the ghost have been Spence Broughton ? Amanda could not tell if he wore old-fashioned clothes or not.

Attercliffe

....

IN THE SEVENTEENTH CENTURY, when Attercliffe was a small country village, we learn from Gatty's *Hallamshire*: 'On July 21st 1661 near Sheffield by the River Don was seen a great army of white soldiers upon the earth; after them went another great multitude of horsemen all in white with white horses. After appearing nearly an hour they all vanished away. Attested by many credible persons. Mr Bloom, formerly Minister of Attercliffe, near Sheffield, where the sight was seen, having examined some neighbours and living in the town, told me of it.'

Victory WMC

73 Darnall Road, Attercliffe

THIS BRICK BUILDING dates from the turn of the century, when it was known as Clifton House and belonged to a doctor.

It is said that the ghost is of a man who died there, but whether of the doctor himself or of a patient is not known. From 1930 it was used by the Darnall Aqueduct Working Men's Club and the ghost first appeared about 1962.

From 1978, the building was taken over by the Victory Working Men's Club. The back part of the building, including the living quarters and snooker room, is original, but the front part has been modernised.

The secretary, Kenneth Elliott, vividly described the goings-on from 1980 in particular. Doors opened and closed by themselves, cold winds whistled about the place, glasses jumped off tables and smashed on the floor.

The steward's dog barked at the door of the snooker room, so the steward opened the door to let him in. The dog was in the room for only four seconds before he shot out, yelping, tail between his legs, absolutely terrified. The room was empty. The dog would not go in again.

A stewardess was eating a sandwich at the bar, when she had to serve a man. She left the sandwich at the back of the bar. Mr Elliott saw the cellar door, which is on a spring, open and close faster than seemed humanly possible. When the stewardess returned for her sandwich, it was gone! A man using the gent's toilet looked into the mirror and saw another man standing behind him. Yet he was alone in the room!

Unfortunately, from the ghost-hunter's point of view, things are quiet nowadays at the club. Dave Clark, there from 1991 experienced nothing unusual.

Aurora Sports Club

Bawtry Road

THE CLUB HOUSE was built just after the Second World War on farmland, intended as a recreational area for the employees of Edgar Allen & Co. Ltd, the steel manufacturers. Since Edgar Allen's became part of the Aurora group of companies, it has been renamed and is now run as a private club for the employees.

There have been two tragedies connected with the club. Some years ago, a non-member, riding past the club on a motor-bike, was involved in an accident and decapitated. More recently, a member playing cricket collapsed and died at the wicket.

In November 1984, a major renovation programme began, and that appears to have been the cause of greater activity by the ghost, who was first seen a year before that by a cleaning lady. She saw him several times since, either just standing around in his dark blue suit or leaning on a pillar. On one occasion her daughter was with her but was unaware of him and he vanished after a few seconds.

On another occasion, the cleaning lady saw him through a glass partition standing in another room. The steward saw the man once.

The secretary, who spent less time in the club house, did not see the man, but around 6th December 1985 he was mending a lock in the ladies' toilets when he heard a scratching noise, apparently coming from a small room behind the toilets, used only during the cricket season and kept locked. Thinking that the steward and stewardess, who live on the premises, were playing a joke, he investigated, but found no-one else in the building, and he later met them coming in after a shopping trip.

A week before that, the cleaning lady

had heard distinct heavy footsteps moving across the club roof.

The ghost especially enjoys playing on the two snooker tables. The secretary saw two or three balls moving about the tables by themselves. Once the steward in his flat below heard balls being struck in the middle of the night. Investigating, he found that balls left in pockets had fallen to the floor. On another occasion when a game was set up, a red ball of its own accord rolled away to rest two feet from the other balls.

On another occasion, before a crowd of onlookers, a player went to hit the white ball and it moved out of his way a foot. The secretary has heard the sounds of a game in progress, but when he went into the room there has been no-one there, though the balls have moved.

The man in the blue suit is still seen regularly. In early 1994, manager Tony Harper felt him waft past. He still plays snooker.

I.R. Tools

41 Mowbray Street, 3
·················

THE FIRM OF I.R. TOOLS, saw manufacturers, was owned by Mr Gagan and later by his daughter.

Mr Gagan used to limp and walked with a stick. Even after his death, he liked to check that all was well. His footsteps could be heard especially in the early morning.

One morning in 1983, Janet Shaw went in first to open up the office. She found the electric kettle boiling away. She shouted: 'Thank you for putting the kettle on!' Then she heard the limping footsteps upstairs. The kettle switched itself off, but she fled outside to wait for her workmate to arrive before she dared go inside again.

Fitzhubert Road

Manor Estate
·····································

JANET SHAW described how, when she lived on Fitzhubert Road, the little boy next door had an imaginary friend called Peter.

One night Janet woke up to see a beautiful little blond boy dressed in white beside her bed. He did not speak, but somehow she knew that he was called Peter. She felt as if she were being pulled inside the bed, but she could not scream.

In that house, doors, especially the living-room door, opened and closed by themselves.

Fretson Road

Manor Estate
·····························

FRANK TOMLINSON died on 11th September 1986. In November his wife, Janet was watching television at 11.30 at night, when Frank walked past behind the settee on which she was sitting, not looking at her, and disappeared. He had told her before he died that he would come back to visit her. However, his ghost was not as clear as in real life but a rather faded image.

Claywood

Sheffield 2
·····················

GILLIAN BONSALL told how for six years, since moving into their mult-storied flat at Claywood, she had been aware of their highwayman ghost.

Her husband had never seen him. The ghost is dressed in black with a white, frilled shirt and a tricorne hat. He smokes a clay pipe, which she can usually smell.

On one occasion, when she was about to get changed, the ghost picked up her skirt from the settee. Kettles and cushions are regularly moved around, presumably by the ghostly hand. Fortunately he seems to be friendly, as she has seen his reflection in the glass of a 1940s china cabinet and in the bath taps.

Croft House Settlement

Garden Street

···

CROFT HOUSE SETTLEMENT is housed in what was once the poorest part of the city and owes its origin to the union of the old Garden Street Congregational Church and Queen Street Church.

It was founded in 1902 by the Reverend W. Blackshaw as a Bible class but provided food and clothes for thousands. It had a house of residence for women with a warden, and began with clubs for fishing, swimming, football, cricket and running.

Outdoor services were held in the neighbouring courts in good weather because the poor, who could not afford a set of best clothes, were shy of attending indoor services. Now it has a thriving operatic society and clubs for boxing, judo and weight-training as well as clog dancing and there is an over-sixties group – a sign of the changing times.

Sister Edith Spencer was the best-known warden, from 1914 to 1939. She dedicated her life to helping youngsters after her fiancée was killed in the First World War, yet died alone and friendless in Firvale Infirmary, aged over eighty.

During the Second World War it became a Services' Club. In 1945 it again became a boys' club with no permanent residents. The white-clad ghost of a lady is said to wander along the passages, mourning her baby who died in a room now kept locked. She is usually seen at night, though once in daylight. She was certainly once seen by cleaners.

The building, which used to be the Congregational Church, mostly dates from the re-building in 1866, when the Reverend Robert Stainton (1825-90) was pastor. He used to preach to the working classes in the *Albert Hall*. Since 1962 the front part of the ground floor has been considerably altered and modernised, with the result that the white lady has apparently been driven away. Only the distant bangings of doors and other odd sounds are heard. Can these be attributed to draughts and the age of the building?

Crookes

Elgin Street

·····················

MR A. UDEN TOLD how his family had lived happily in their mock-Tudor semi for seven years until they bought a piano for their nine-year-old daughter. Her piano teacher said there was no point in carrying on with her lessons unless she practised at home. However, she stubbornly refused to do, which led to some terrible family rows.

One day during a row a loud knocking began on the dividing wall. It continued for half an hour in a constant rhythm. Every time a row started, the knocking began. They thought it was the neighbours. However, when the knocking was mentioned to the neighbours, it turned out that they had thought the Udens were responsible.

They invited a clairvoyant to the house. She told them: 'It's the old man, who used to live here, he doesn't like all the noise. You won't get it any more.' And they never did.

Argyll House

Williamson Road, Sharrow
....

T HIS BLEAK RAMBLING Victorian mansion was left in trust to Nether Edge Hospital in 1950 and used as a nurses' home. From about 1954 it had the reputation of being haunted by a Lady in Grey. A cleaner heard strange knocking noises and

a decorator opened a door and saw the ghost standing in the corner of a room. He hurriedly slammed the door. When he gathered up his courage to open it again, the ghost was gone.

Since 1991 Argyll House has been used as a community mental health centre and on one day a week is a drop-in centre for mentally handicapped people. The ghost has not been seen in recent years.

Sheffield Twist Drill

Sharrow
....

S HEFFIELD TWIST DRILL and Steel Company was founded in 1913 at the corner of Summerfield Street and Napier Street.

It had three operating divisions, the Dormer Tools Division responsible for the manufacture and marketing of different types and sizes (presently 24,000) of standard twist drills, reamers, end mills and thread-cutting tools.

In 1975 it was bought by SKF Swedish bearing manufacturers, being renamed SKF at Dormer. In 1989 a new factory was built on Rother Valley Way, Holbrook, the old factory being pulled down in 1995.

In 1993 it was sold to another Swedish company, Sandvik and renamed Dormer Tools Ltd. The company currently employs 450 people, mostly in Sheffield but also at two small locations in the Midlands.

A Mr Tingle was working on the Summerfield Street factory, when it was first built and was killed in an accident.

An employee described how he was in the inspection area, when he saw a man in a brown smock run across a corridor and vanish into thin air. Six women were clocking out at the time, but their backs were to the slope up to the corridor and they did not see anything.

Mount Pleasant

Sharrow Lane
·······························

THIS LARGE RED-BRICK building just off London Road was built by Francis Hurt Sitwell in 1786. Francis Hurt inherited half a million pounds from his uncle, William Sitwell of Renishaw. He took the Sitwell arms and name in 1771 by Royal sign-manual, inheriting Renishaw through his mother, Catherine Sitwell.

In 1794 the Sitwells sold Mount Pleasant to Samuel Broomhead Ward.

The original house on the site is said to have been built by a nobleman for his new bride. Haughtily, she told him, 'Indeed, an' it is not so grand a place as my father's stables – I'd scorn to live within its walls.'

In fact that house was much added onto. After the Wards it was owned by various families until 1868, when it was leased for five years as a lunatic asylum.

In 1874 it was taken over by a girls' charity school, which had moved from St James Row. This became the Mount Pleasant School for Girls in 1927.

After World War II it was used by various government departments, such as the Ministries of Fuel and Transport and the Ministry of Works Engineering Division. By 1961 there was just the National Assistance Board in the house and the Driving Examiners Department in the old coach house. When all the government departments finally left, it deteriorated.

Thankfully it has now been restored for use as a community centre with a youth club in the coach house.

Like any self-respecting old house, Mount Pleasant has its ghosts – a woman witness described how it seemed as if a door opened and suddenly there was the sound of many children's voices before the door closed again.

In 1987, seventy-five-year-old Mr F.

Brown told how as a joiner with the Sheffield Public Works Department he went to dismantle vandalised fittings at what was then Sitwell House.

One afternoon, about one-thirty he was repairing a door in the ground floor hall when he heard from upstairs the sound of running and jumping feet, though he heard no voices.

He ran upstairs, but could not find anyone. No-one could have left the upstairs room without his seeing them. Then he realised that no-one could have run around, because the rough floorboards were covered with rubble and broken glass.

Highfield

Bennett Street
·····················

A GENTLEMAN TOLD how in 1975 his grandparents lived in No.8 and rented out No.10. His grandmother died and his grandfather moved into an old folks' home. His grandmother had had a long wall clock. Whenever anyone became upset, his grandmother grew agitated and the clock would fly open.

The grandson stayed on in No.10 until it was compulsorily purchased and subsequently demolished by the council. One night a friend stayed there. In the morning he was still shaking, when he told how Gran's ghost had come through the wall from next door to inspect him.

Heeley Bridge

London Road
·····························

THERE WAS A BRIDGE at Heeley as far back as the Norman Conquest, but the early bridge stood higher upstream

just below the confluence of the Meersbrook and the Sheaf, almost opposite the bottom of Gleadless Road. It was referred to in the accounts of the Capital Burgesses in 1566: *'Towards the makynge of Heeley Bridge XXs* (20 shillings)'.

The ghost of a woman is said to walk through a wall of the bridge. She may be re-enacting a tragedy, which took place between the First and Second World Wars. At that time before the building of the Norton Lees estate in the later thirties, the water level at Heeley Bridge was much deeper than now, when the rainwater runs away into street drains rather than down the hill into the river.

The woman, in a state of mental distress, murdered her two children and was sent to prison. When she was released, she jumped from Heeley Bridge and drowned.

Heeley

Cutlers' Bridge

••••••••••••••••

ON JUNE 26TH 1668, John Bowman, a tailor of Greenhill, then a village in Derbyshire, made a deposition before a magistrate at York, Francis Barber, Esq.

He said that on the Tuesday before Ascension Day he was coming home about midday from the market in the small town of Sheffield. As he walked along the footway towards Heeley (then called Highley), which was a separate village, he was overtaken by his friend John Brumhead and they carried on together to Cutler's Bridge (where Bramall Lane and Myrtle Road meet).

They were talking idly of an apparition which folk had seen there, of a man they called Earl George. Even as they were speaking, a man suddenly appeared before them, dressed like a prince with a green doublet and ruff and holding a brachete, a hound bitch, in his hands. It would seem that John Brumheed took to his heels. John Bowman lay in a dead faint for half an hour. When he awoke, he saw a man passing him with two laden horses and was glad to have his company on the remainder of the road into Heeley.

'Earl George' was undoubtedly George Talbot, sixth Earl of Shrewsbury, the richest and most powerful peer in England. A well-known figure in the Sheffield area in his lifetime, his especial connection with Cutler's Bridge can only be conjectured. The hound bitch in his hands suggests that he hunted there in the days when The Moor really was moorland.

Born in 1528, he married in 1568 the formidable Bess of Hardwick. In 1571-72 he was appointed Lord High Steward of England and Earl Marshall.

As he owned the strongly-built Sheffield Castle, Elizabeth I made him custodian of Mary, Queen of Scots.

At first Bess and Mary were quite friendly, but later Bess became jealous of her husband's friendship with his prisoner. Also she wanted her grand-daughter, Arabella Stuart, to succeed to the throne. So she told her sons, William and Charles Cavendish, to spread rumours that their stepfather, whom they disliked, was having an affair with Mary.

Soon rumours credited Mary with having had at least two children by the Earl. When Mary protested Elizabeth intervened and officially exonerated him. Bess and her sons soon found it prudent to issue official denials. The Earl could not forgive Bess and their marriage broke up. In 1584 he was relieved of his custodianship of Mary, and in 1587 assisted at her execution.

After a year in London he retired to the small mansion in Handsworth, (the now demolished Handsworth Hall Farm on Finchwell Crescent) which he had built in 1577, for he was now crippled with gout. On 18th November 1590 he died at Manor Castle. His sumptuous funeral, with many great lords and ladies attending, was the talk of the town for years afterwards.

Heeley Baths

Broadfield Road 7

I N JUNE 1907 the Local Government Board held an inquiry into the desirability of building public baths at Heeley, to serve a rapidly expanding population, many of whom lived in back-to-back and terraced houses with toilets across the back yards. Bathrooms were luxuries enjoyed by the well-to-do. Poorer folk made do with a tin bath in front of the fire.

The baths actually opened on July 20th 1909. Swimmers were charged 2d a session, for use of the slipper baths 3d and for the Russian baths – especially recommended for rheumatics – 6d.

A booklet from the 1950s tells of parties of schoolchildren going free during school hours for swimming lessons by qualified instructors.

There was mixed bathing on Thursdays 1-8 pm and Ladies Only sessions on Tuesdays and Fridays 2-8 pm. In the Russian baths there were 'Men Only' sessions on Monday, Wednesday, Thursday and Saturday and 'Ladies Only' on Tuesday and Friday.

The public wash-house adjoining offered washing-machines, hand washing stalls and dryers.

A 1997 leaflet offers swimming sessions every day including Sunday – a sign of the times. Other activities include aqua keep-fit, early morning swimming, fun sessions, junior and adult lessons, over 50's, parent and toddler and women only sessions.

The baths are said to be haunted by two ghosts, one a man who died in the slipper baths and the other, a workman, who was killed in an accident.

Bed (The Music Factory)

London Road, Sharrow

O N THE CORNER OF London Road and Boston Road (formerly Street) there used to be a row of small shops. In 1913, No.41 was occupied by Reuben Short, tripe dealer, No.43 by William Plowright, marine store dealer, No.45 by John Lowe, outfitter and hosier and No.47 by Henry Wilkinson, hairdresser.

The following year these were all swept away in favour of an imposing white building surmounted by a cupola, which was designed by W.G. Buck.

On the 18th December 1914 it opened as the *Lansdowne Picture Palace*. Its original seating capacity was 1500, but this gradually fell to 965 in 1940, when it closed on 12th December.

The bomb damage it suffered during the Blitz was slight, but Lansdowne Pictures Ltd were doubtless relieved to receive an offer too good to refuse from Marks and Spencer.

It remained a department store until 1954, when it was bought by Mecca. The Locarno Ballroom was very popular. It was succeeded by Tiffany's Dance Hall, The Palais, and then the Locarno Night Club. It then became one of the top northern night clubs, The Music Factory.

After closing for two months, it reopened in October 1998 as Club Generation, lasting only until April 1999, when its owners went into receivership. It was then bought by the Gatecrasher organisation and is now the nightclub Bed.

The building is said to be haunted by a young woman, who fell from the balcony stairs while carrying a tray of drinks.

Other stories involve a customer, who hung himself in the toilets and some tramps, who were found dead in the cellar after the bombing in 1940. The one certainty is that over the years many people have been driven out of the cellar, convinced that they were being chased by a ghost, although no-one has actually seen anything. They all report sensing a Presence and feeling an unnatural coldness. The coldness has been felt only by cleaners and other staff during the daytime and after the customers have left at 2 am. Perhaps the ghost or ghosts prefer to hide away from noisy customers.

Silver Blades Ice Rink
Queens Road
··

BETWEEN FARM ROAD and Duchess Road, the ice rink is part of a complex, which includes a casino and a bingo hall.

It was built by Mecca Ltd on land which in 1884 was the Belle Vue Bowling Green. In about 1919 the Municipal Tuberculosis Dispensary was built there with John Rennie, MD Medical Officer in charge. By 1961 this had become the Sheffield Chest Clinic.

The leisure complex was constructed in 1965. The ice rink was opened on November 30th by the Lord Mayor – Alderman J.S. Worrall – with a pair of scissors shaped like skating blades. It was open to the public from December 2nd with three skating sessions daily. A restaurant overlooked the ice rink and at the rink side was the Milky Way refreshment bar and the 'Heart Beat', where one could dine and dance. An ice machine was imported from USA at a cost of £7,000.

It is now called the Sheffield Ice Sports Centre and is home to several clubs, Sheffield Ice Racing Club for speed skaters, Sheffield and Hallamshire Ice Dance and Free Skating Club, and Hallamshire Advanced Skating College. Sheffield Ice Hockey Club is affiliated to the very successful professional Sheffield Steelers, who occasionally use the rink for training.

The ice rink is reputed to be haunted by a woman, who may have been a TB patient, though Steve Scott, manager in 1974, admitted that mist arising from the ice at night can create strange shapes. A woman employee, no longer working there, described a woman entering by the door at the back of the rink, walking around to the right hand side and then disappearing into thin air. This apparition has been seen by other people in the same place. On one occasion a customer saw through the glass doors a male figure in Victorian costume in the refreshment area, but on opening the doors, found no-one there.

Gleadless Valley

Leighton Road
....

AUDREY GILL, a practical down-to-earth girl, was seventeen years old in 1975 when she first saw her 'little green man'. She was coming out of the bathroom, when she saw the little gnome, with his greenish skin, green pointed cap, green jerkin and green buckled shoes, cheeky face alight with merriment, laughing at her from the bottom of the stairs. That first time she was rather frightened, but as she saw him several times more at the same spot and realised that he meant her no harm, she grew quite fond of him, telling the rest of her family not to laugh. Her little green man did exist and he was bringing her good luck. Indeed her father once caught a glimpse of him. Something small and green flashed past him. As her mother pointed out, gnomes do move very fast. Her mother, to her own regret, never saw him. Audrey is religious, but although her Church teaches that gnomes and other such creatures do not exist, she knows what she has seen, and also that after the first time she saw him, her luck seemed to change. Among other things, she was promoted to manageress.

Her mother consulted a clairvoyant, who told her that their council house, built in 1960, was on the site of woodland and farmland. Part of the woods in fact still exist, and were the homes of fairies and gnomes. She should put out a saucer of milk each day for their little guest.

Audrey married and moved to Lincoln.

The little green man moved with her and continued to bring her luck. When her son, Christopher was about two years old, he would point to the top of his wardrobe and tell them that a little man was sitting there. No-one else saw him in Lincoln until March 1984, when Audrey woke one morning after her husband had got up, to find the gnome sitting beside her bed. Over the years he had aged and grown a beard! A week later they had the luck to obtain a house in Sheffield, but perhaps the gnome was too old to travel back with them. They have had much bad luck since.

Gleadless

Hang Bank Wood
....

ARMITAGE'S *Chantrey Land* perpetuates the legend that Hang Bank Wood, called locally Cat Lane Wood, which hugs the bank of the Meersbrook below Callow Mount flats, is haunted by the ghost of a man who hanged himself there. Harrison's 1637 survey of Sheffield describes a pasture that 'abutteth upon Newfield greene North and a Common called Hanbanke South'. Strictly speaking it was Buck Wood where he hanged himself, but by an association of ideas the name changed over the years.

In the poem of John Holland (1794-1873) we read:

Forgetful of thy haunted glen, Lees Hall!

Through which we hasted homeward

Despite the almost unearthly stillness, common to most woods, which the city-dweller, used to the constant roar of traffic, finds unnerving, there were apparently no sightings of the unhappy suicide for many years. Perhaps he was driven away by housing developments impinging upon his wood. Perhaps the hanging tree was cut

Traces of Ancient Beliefs

THE MEERSBROOK at Heeley, now culverted for part of its length, was not so many years ago the old boundary between Yorkshire and Derbyshire. In earlier times it marked the boundary between Northumbria, held by the Vikings, and Mercia. Legends in the Sheffield area reflect the mixture of Norse and Celtic beliefs, together with older native ones.

Long after the Celts conquered the whole of north Britain and became nominally Christian, their lives were still ruled by older beliefs. Their Christian faith itself was riddled with memories of pagan rituals.

A BBC2 programme reported that a community of between two and three hundred people on scattered farms and smallholdings in the High Peak district of Derbyshire still practice the ancient Celtic religion. They are very secretive, but believe in the Earth Mother, the Horned God and other pagan deities. They hold rites to ensure the fertility of their crops, but these do not have the sexual overtones as were once practised. Dr Anne Ross of Southampton University believes that the Celtic, not the Anglo-Saxon religion is the true source of present-day customs and traditions.

Fairies, witches and the spirits of the dead were always lying in wait to carry off the unwary. The very name of Ecclesall is probably derived from *Hecksel-Hallr* meaning witches' hill; Dobbin Hill is from the northern word *Dobby* meaning a goblin; and Endcliffe was originally Elcliffe, the elf bank or cliff.

Fairies were supposed to live in the fireplace and Derbyshire housewives would clean the hearth before going to bed, to make the fairies comfortable. They were supposed to bring good luck to the household and it was wise to avoid offending them. There are various theories about the legends of fairies. Were they folk-memories of the small, dark Stone Age peoples who once lived in Britain and were driven by the Celts into hiding in woods, remote hills and caves; were they memories of ancient pagan gods and nature spirits or early attempts to explain the activities of poltergeists?

After Elizabeth I's time there was a decline in the belief in fairies and few modern accounts of them. The photographs of the fairies from Cottingley near Bradford, taken at the end of the First World War, were denounced as fakes, though experts could not explain how they were faked.

Nowadays, people are shy of admitting that they believe in fairies, but that does not stop them saluting 'the little people' as they pass over Ballona Bridge on the Douglas to Castletown road on the Isle of Man. Perhaps they have an inner reservation that it is better to be safe than sorry. No-one, however, could have been more amazed than the Sheffield couple driving down a quiet country lane in Cornwall, who saw a pixie in pointed cap, green jerkin and buckled shoes pop out for a second or two from behind a hedge. He was about three foot in height. Another couple driving along a lonely Scottish road saw a tiny man and a woman, whom they also described as pixies, cross the road in front of them. When they returned home to Sheffield, their experiences must have seemed as distant as dreams. Such things maybe did happen in remote parts of the country, but not in a large industrial city.

Little did they know!

down. Or had he come to the end of his ghostly life-span? It is said that even ghosts gradually fade away after about three or four hundred years, though it is firmly believed by many people that Roman soldiers still roam the Rivelin Valley.

A ship's steward described how, as a young child, he wandered into the woods by himself and saw, coming towards him, a vague figure in white, floating several feet off the ground. At the time, being too young to understand, he was not afraid, but there was something unusual about it that made him remember it years later, though now it seems as if it was in a dream.

Meersbrook

Albert Road
....

I
N THE SUMMER OF 1987, Andy Starbuck was renting a back bedroom in an old house on Albert Road. It was six-thirty in the evening. The friend who was with him was looking in the direction of the open windows with their open curtains. Andy, facing the opposite direction, saw the head of an old man, bearded and wearing a fisherman's sou'wester in the manner of Captain Birdseye, float very fast across the back right-hand corner of the room near the ceiling and disappear.

Bishops' House

Meersbrook Park
....

B
ISHOPS' HOUSE at the top of Meersbrook Park is the most complete example of a timber-framed house to survive in Sheffield. The original builders and owners are unknown, but it was built about 1500.

There is a strong local tradition that two brothers lived there, John Blythe, who was Bishop of Salisbury from 1494 to 1499 and Geoffrey Blythe, who was Bishop of Lichfield and Coventry from 1503 to 1533. There is in fact no documentary evidence of this and the name 'Bishops' House' is of recent origin. The Blythes, however, did own land and property locally from at least the fourteenth century, and one branch of the family certainly lived at the house in the 1600s. William Blythe was a captain with the Parliamentary army in the Civil War and helped to supervise the demolition of Sheffield Castle. He was also a prosperous farmer and miller, and organiser of scythe manufacture and trade.

The house is not large enough to have belonged to anyone other than one of the minor gentry or a prosperous yeoman farmer. There were once barns and other outbuildings attached. Between 1500 and 1700 there were many alterations and improvements but many original features can still be seen.

In 1753 the house was sold and the new owners divided it into two dwellings, but no major alterations were made apart from internal partitions and some doors and windows being added. Up to 1974 it housed park employees, when it was decided to turn it into a museum. After extensive restoration and repairs, it was opened to the public in 1976 and so successful has it been that in 1978 it received a plaque and a special commendation as a finalist for the Museum of the Year award.

The house is furnished in sixteenth-century style, but unfortunately not with the original furniture, as far as is known. Most pieces were taken from the City Museum collection, among them being a certain oak jewellery box.

The plain polished object stands on a cabinet beside the bed. Its history is unknown, nor how it came into the City Museum collection, but it is at least 300 years old. The casual visitor is inclined to

overlook it in favour of more spectacular objects, but to those in the know it is the most interesting exhibit in the house.

The box is always kept locked, and the key is stored at Weston Park Museum. Staff have struggled in vain to open it once it has been locked, so they are certain that the lock is not faulty. Yet at frequent but irregular intervals it has been found unlocked. The curator is sure that no visitors have tampered with it, as on many occasions it has been checked and found to be locked after all the visitors have gone and the staff are preparing to go home for the night – yet in the morning when they come on duty it is found inexplicably unlocked!

In 1997, when a colleague was upstairs polishing the box, John Herbert sensed a strange presence behind him, but there was no-one there. Now he believes it is best not to polish it, just to give it a gentle dusting.

In June 1983 a medium visiting the museum sensed a presence in the bedroom. Footsteps have been heard in the entrance hall, when there was no-one else there, also a whistling outside, when there was no-one to be seen.

Gregory Howard, after working there for ten years, experienced nothing, but dogs refuse to walk past the house. Perhaps they see the White Lady. In 1992 a couple sitting on the wall near the park entrance in the summer evening were astonished to see her walk into the house through a doorway (just above the present main entrance) which has been blocked up, for security reasons, since the house became a museum. During that same summer two elderly gentlemen were leaning on the wall chatting, about nine in the evening, when they saw her enter the house through the wall on the other side of the house. Then in 1993 a gentleman looked over the wall from Lees Nook and saw her walking down past the house on the grass verge next to the wall. On November 5th 1991 at 3am a taxi driver was walking his dog in the park, when he saw her standing against the railings by the toilets, looking towards the city.

In the Spring of 1984 a boy and his dog, Sam, chased the White Lady in the section of the park between the allotments and the terraced houses.

Woodseats Palace
692 Chesterfield Road
....

AFFECTIONATELY KNOWN AS 't'Bug 'Ut', the Woodseats Palace opened on September 4th 1911. Its architect was William A. Forsdike.

In 1911, its seating capacity was 550. This was increased to 800 in 1921, reflecting the growing popularity of cinemagoing. However, by 1935, it seated only 640 and in 1954, 617.

At first, its owners were the Woodseats Palace Co. Ltd, but from 1920 it was owned by Heeley and Amalgamated Cinemas Ltd. From January 1955 it was the property of Star Cinemas Ltd.

By 1961, people were staying at home to watch television. The Woodseats Palace finally closed on September 24th.

The building was converted into a supermarket. It had a succession of owners until Alldays opened in June 1998 and closed on 8th December 1999. At present it lays empty.

The history of the ghost is unknown. We only know that she is a woman, who was seen by several members of the Alldays staff on the first floor although never in the shop. Some staff refused to go upstairs at night. She banged about and slammed doors, and even called them by name.

Radio Sheffield

Westbourne Road, Broomhill.

····································

ASHDELL GROVE, Westbourne Road, the home of Radio Sheffield, is a listed building. It was built in the 1860s as the town house of the Manager of Tennants' Brewery.

As befits its status, the rambling old house has its resident ghost, who in 1970 was, it is said, responsible for taking Radio Sheffield off the air, when a control knob mysteriously closed.

According to an ex-police superintendent it is the ghost of a maid who around 1908 was courting a constable. She would wait until the gentlemen of the house had retired to the library after dinner. Then she would walk down the cellar steps and through a door to a rendezvous with her boyfriend in the orchard.

The ghost is indeed dressed in a maid's outfit with black stockings, cap and apron. She is of human form except for her face, which is lined with little squares like a television picture.

When the house was used by a government department, Norman Savage of Crosspool saw what had the appearance of a chambermaid four times during 1960 and 1961. Mr Savage said it would appear from the middle of November to the end of January and then not be seen until the following winter. He and others who had seen it were sworn to secrecy for fear that staff would panic and refuse to work there at night.

Since Radio Sheffield moved in, with its first broadcast on 15th November 1967, people have seen unaccountable things, but all agree that the ghost seems to be benevolent. Gerry Kersey often worked there into the early hours of the morning. Once as he passed a cupboard, the door suddenly opened and tape spools came out as if being thrown. He flung the door wide open but no-one was there. Once at 2 am he looked up from editing a tape and saw a shadow pass by the window in the door, but he was alone in the building.

In August 1978, Phil Baldry finished a late news shift. He went to the door of the news room from which he could see the main stairway and an archway. A white form fluttered across the archway. Shaken, he switched out all the lights, and left by the glass panelled front door. The glass panels reflected the street lights. As he double-locked the door, he saw reflected in the door panel the face of an old man. Phil was young. He fled.

In January 1980, twenty ghoul hunters from psychic research groups came from Preston and Manchester as well as Sheffield with video and recording equipment to watch all night, but the elusive chambermaid was stricken with stage-fright and declined to appear before such a large audience.

In January 1996, Clare, a member of staff, entered room SPA. She glanced through the window, which covered most of the wall dividing it from studio 1A, and saw a shadowy figure in the corner near the outside window. At first she thought there was someone in the room, then it disappeared and she realised she had seen the resident ghost.

In March 1996 it was decided to turn an upstairs room into another office. Someone opened a supposed cupboard door and found a long-forgotten Victorian wrought-iron spiral staircase, which led into an attic, probably the very room where

house. It is completely dark and deserted. I was up there one day changing the frequency. I'm really sceptical about ghosts, but I felt something touch my shoulder and I was out of there like a shot.'

Oakhill Road

Nether Edge,
....

A LADY NOW LIVING IN Plymouth, Beryl Browitt described what happened when she lived in Nether Edge.

The 'Thing' first appeared in 1976 when she was pregnant and suffering a difficult confinement which kept her awake at night. On a number of occasions she saw a shapeless mass in her bedroom, like mist or smoke at the centre of which were tiny pulsating lights. It swirled like cigar smoke and continued to drift in the air for lengthy periods, while the air in the room felt unusually cold.

Other people saw it too, though never as often as Mrs Browitt, who experienced a feeling of peace and calm each time. One woman, who walked into the bedroom, felt the hairs on her arms stand on end and tingle as though affected by static electricity. There were several mysterious failures of electrical equipment in the room.

The 'Thing' followed her to Plymouth, though she saw it only once there. A visitor there, who knew nothing about it, entered her bedroom but came out quickly, saying she could not stop in there because there was something frightening. However, it did not bother Mrs Browitt, who said it made her feel calm and happy.

Mrs Browitt has also seen a UFO in Abbeydale Road, a sighting confirmed by other witnesses, including police officers.

the maidservant had slept, and then via a plain wooden staircase onto the roof.

Radio Sheffield holds the building from Sheffield City Council on a lease. The hard-up council plans to sell it after Radio Sheffield moved to a brand new building on Paternoster Row in mid-2001. Fortunately, as Ashdell Grove is a listed building, it cannot be pulled down.

105 FM

Kenwood Park Road, Nether Edge
....

T HE PIRATE RADIO STATION 105 FM closed down in July 1997, when officials from the Department of Trade and Industry raided the seven-bedroomed 18th century house from which it was transmitting.

The station bosses were secretly relieved to have been moved out of the old home of the 18th century 'Kenwood Park killer'. He came home one day to find his wife in the arms of another man. Enraged, he chopped off her head with an axe.

A 105 FM spokesman said: 'A couple of strange things happened to us in the

Swallow Hotel

Kenwood Road, Nether Edge
··································

T HE HOTEL STANDS on land, which in 1100 AD belonged to the Priory of Worksop, to which its founder, William de Lovetot, Lord of the Manor of Sheffield had granted a third of the tithes. The local farmers paid their tithes with corn and other crops, so a Grange and large barns were built to store them.

After the Dissolution of the Monasteries under Henry VIII the priory land was sold to the Swifts of Broom Hall, who farmed it until 1796.

The well-known cutler George Wostenholm, who developed a flourishing market in America, including the blades for the 'Bowie' knives, built a modern factory in Sheffield, which he called the Washington Works (now demolished). In 1836 he bought land in order to create a park like ones he had seen near Cincinnati.

In 1845 he built Kenwood mansion from Sheffield marble. The main rooms were heavily decorated with much gold leaf and included mirrors which could be wound up through the floor to shutter the windows. The gardens were designed by Robert Marnock, who later designed the Botanical Gardens, and they have changed little since his day with all kinds of shrubs, trees and an ornamental lake. There are many shaded walks. The one around the lake is known as the Gargoyle Walk from the gargoyles guarding it. It was rumoured at the time in Sheffield that Wostenholm had paid for his mansion with the profits from gun-running during the American Civil War.

He had no children from any of his three wives, so the last wife's heiress was Miss Margaret Rundel, who was the last of the family to live at Kenwood. She sold it in 1942 to the Sheffield Café Company (started in 1921), who converted it into a temperance hotel, mainly for long staying guests.

Soon afterwards, the Sheffield Café Company was renamed Sheffield Refreshment Houses who also bought the Omega Restaurant, Hunter House Hotel, Harley Commercial Hotel, St Andrew's Hotel and Roslyn Court Hotel.

In 1958 the banqueting suite, Kenwood Hall was built, and in 1975 the adjacent four-star Hotel St George within the park.

Swallow Hotels have owned the complex since November 1982 and in the following autumn completed the link-up between the two hotels. Kenwood was renamed the Swallow Hotel.

It is the older Kenwood building, which is described as spooky. The ducks on the lake only venture near the hotel at breakfast time. Light switches go on and off by themselves in the main bar. Ashtrays fall off tables. Telephones ring when there is no-one on the line.

Abbeydale Picture House

Abbeydale Road
··································

I N THE HEYDAY OF cinema-going between the two world wars, Sheffield had forty-five cinemas, mostly showing different films, unlike now when low-budget films struggle to get a showing anywhere.

All the original cinemas are now closed and, if not demolished, have been converted to bingo halls or for industrial purposes.

Abbeydale Picture House was the only Sheffield cinema to become a listed building. There was a café at balcony level with a ballroom and a billiard hall in the basement. Its architect was Arthur Whitaker of Dixon and Stienlet.

It opened on 20th December 1920 with an audience capacity of 1560 by 1935. The original proprietors were Abbeydale Picture House Ltd and from 1955 Star Cinemas. Music for silent films was played on a Clavorchestra, an orchestral organ built by Charles Brindley of Sheffield.

Television's growing popularity forced many cinemas to close and on 5th July 1975 the Abbeydale followed suit.

The building was later used as the office equipment showrooms of A. and F. Drake until 1991, when it again became empty except for a snooker club in the basement. The Speakeasy club then had part of the building with live bands, satellite TV, a juke box and discos presided over by a DJ. It then became the Bar Abbey.

Abbeydale Road

....

ARE THE CELTS more open to other-worldly contacts than other races? Irish builder, Mick Flynn is convinced of this, after the various experiences of members of his own family.

He once owned a house in Abbeydale Road, which he rented out. When it became vacant, a friend's daughter, moving from Wales, arranged to rent it. Mick and his son, Michael were decorating it. They were emulsioning the landing when the air suddenly became cold. Nick saw a featureless head and body with no arms or legs floating up the attic stairs in a cloud of smoke. His son saw only a bit of mist.

The daughter moved in. One day her mother was waiting in the sitting-room to go with her to the laundrette, when an icy blast went through the room. The daughter decided to return to Wales after only a month or two. Mick went for the key. He found her ironing in the back bedroom with the ghost at her side!

The caretaker at the Cutlers' Hall rented it for a short while. He asked Mick if any murders had been committed in the house. His son, aged six, was too frightened to sleep in the attic. His daughter, aged seven, slept there and saw the ghost. Mick's daughter, Catherine went to live there. Something grabbed her in bed and held her leg.

Mick sold the house in 1976.

In May 1975, Mick was at a friend's house in Binfield Road, Meersbrook. The friend was looking after the next door house while the owner was on holiday. Mick went out with his friend. When they returned, the friend's wife, who had been reading in bed, said she had heard banging from next door. The men went to investigate, but found nothing. They returned to the wife, who insisted that she had heard the banging again, while they had been next door. Mick went back next door on his own, but still found nothing.

Eighteen months previously he had done some major renovation at his friend's house. Whlle working there he had kept his tools in a cubby hole up the attic stairs. He remarked how icy cold the cubby hole was. A few weeks after the banging incident his friend called him to check the electricity, because the television turned itself on and lights would go on and off by themselves. Mick was at the house one Sunday afternoon, when the three girls, aged 12, 6 and 3 and the boy aged 10 were not at home. He and the lady of the house, drinking coffee in the sitting-room, heard light footsteps, as of a young person, running overhead from the front wall to the back, as if passing through the wall, not through the door at the side of the bedroom.

The two eldest girls slept in the attic. One night the girls ran downstairs screaming. A dress belonging to the eldest was hanging on a hook on one wall. It suddenly flew across the room and stuck to the wall opposite.

The boy slept in a bedroom with a glass door panel. Through it he saw the silhouette of a strange man. He sometimes awoke feeling a presence in the room with him. On several occasions he saw a man at the foot of his bed, wearing a cloak and a Spanish type hat with a wide brim. The youngest and eldest girls did not see the man, but the middle girl did. All these incidents took place over one year.

A young couple were the next occupants. They brought with them from South Africa a heavy carved dining table. The ghost turned the table upside down. They too felt the icy coldness of the cubby hole, saw the man in the cloak, had the lights switching themselves on and off and also had articles flying about the rooms and getting broken.

Mick's daughter, Jackie wouldn't stay at her father's house in Springfield Road. The grandchildren refused to go upstairs.

Jackie once saw something like a ball of fire at the bottom of her bed. Mick's mother was staying in the back room after a stroke. She saw someone at the foot of her bed with his head under his arm.

She went into a nursing home. On a visit she gave Mick a family photograph to keep at home. It was of his father and mother and a cousin, taken in the *Barrel*

Inn, London Road in 1947. Mick put it on his sideboard. His grandson then aged eight had never seen his great-grandfather or a photograph of him, as his great-grandfather had died in 1957. He did not know that his great-grandfather's name was Flynn. He pointed to the photograph and said 'Oh, it's Mr Flynn. He comes to see me at night and talks to me.'

When she and her family went to live at Scunthorpe, Mick's daughter was told at a séance that her grandfather was fighting to protect the family against evil spirits in the Springfield Road house.

Bunting Nook, Norton

....

BUNTING NOOK WAS named after Joseph Bunting, who was born in 1800 and made his fortune in America before returning home to become proprietor of the Norton Green bowling green, which had been used for bowls as long ago as 1681.

The narrow, lonely tree-lined lane has changed little in the past hundred years. Cross-roads are often said to be haunted by boggards, so naturally Bunting Nook, where three roads meet, has its boggard. This particular one is supposed to have the form of a dog.

In 1958 a police officer on night patrol was standing at the bottom of the Nook where it meets Hemsworth Road, when he happened to turn round and saw that about ten yards behind him a patch of mist had formed – mist that was definitely green and human-shaped, about five-foot six-inches in height. As he watched, it dissolved as quickly as it had formed. Uneasy, yet unwilling to consider it as anything more than an unusual mist, he told his colleagues about it when he got back to the station and several of them admitted to having seen it too at the same spot.

In Norton Church yard is a gravestone with the following inscription:

'Sacred to the Memory of Charles, son of Charles and Hannah Glover of Holmhirst, who departed this life, July 5th 1846 aged 16 years.
In evil hour I fell, oppress'd with pain by bloody minded men untimely slain.
O may they find, through Jesus crucified
That mercy their evil hands to me denied'.

It commemorates the murder of the boy in Bunting Nook. He was robbed and clubbed to death by three ruffians. Is it his ghost which now haunts the scene of the crime, or Jack-in-the-Green?

The Boating Lake
Graves Park
....

READERS WILL BE intrigued by the photograph to the right. Do they see what the author and photographer see?

In January 1991 I received a telephone call from a gentleman living at Batemoor and a few days later some photographs by post. In his covering letter the gentlemen explained 'I took the photo looking across Graves Park boating lake to try and capture the reflection of the trees upon the lake and since then have kept putting it away to try and forget about it. I occasionally take it out again to stare at it until it drives me mad so back in the drawer it goes.'

He took the black and white photograph in the middle of October 1989 and developed it himself. At first it seemed unremarkable. Then he spotted something in a gap between some trees. He made an

enlargement and found himself looking at what seemed to be a girl in a long, white, short-sleeved dress, holding a bunch of flowers.

When he took the photo he was careful to check that there were no people within camera range. He would certainly have noticed a girl in a heavily flounced bridal dress. It was a bitterly cold day with a sharp wind. He himself was wearing his thickest anorak. Two weeks later when he took another photograph from the same position, the trees had lost their leaves. He showed me the place at the same time of the year in identical weather. We picked out the trees near the girl. The bottom of her skirt is curiously flat. She could have been walking along a path, which in her time (late Victorian or Edwardian?) was several inches lower than today.

The chairman of the Ghost Club in London, Tom Perrott was sufficiently impressed by the photograph to send it to an American expert, who was convinced that it was not a fake.

So who was the girl? There are two or three possibilities.

About 20 years ago a lady went to a friend's wedding at Norton Parish Church. She arrived before the bridal party so she

passed the time taking photographs of the outside of the church and churchyard. There was no-one else around at the time, so she was astonished to see on the developed photographs the image of an unknown bridesmaid in Victorian or Edwardian costume. She wrote to Kodak who told her that the bridesmaid was familiar to them. She frequently appeared in wedding photographs taken outside Norton Church.

The lady showed the photograph to a friend, who, years later, was shown the photograph of the bridesmaid by the lake. The friend was sure that it was the same girl in both photographs. Unfortunately by then the lady photographer was dead. As she was unmarried, her house had been emptied by distant relatives and the photograph of Norton churchyard, has probably ended up in the dustbin. So, we may never know for sure if it was the same girl – unless some fortunate reader has another photograph of the churchyard ghost.

There is an old story from Oakes Park, which was mentioned in documents dating from 1543. The present house was built about 1670 and completely remodelled in the early 1800s. After nearly 300 years there the Bagshawe family decided to sell it to Henry Boot Ltd, when the building of Bochum Parkway ruined their privacy. It has now been sold to Dan and Billie Thaw, who plan to turn it into a Christian holiday centre for children.

Some time in the last century, during a wedding reception at the house, a messenger came with bad news for the bride. She hurried out across the park and was later found drowned in the lake. The story does not specify which lake. It was more likely to be the ornamental lake at Oakes Park than the boating lake in Graves Park – unless in the telling Oakes Park has been substituted for Norton Hall.

Another story concerns a member of the Shore family of Norton Hall, who is said to

Boggards and Green Men

THE VIKING SETTLERS brought with them tales of ogres, demons and dragons. In the legend of the 'Dragon of Wantley' a dragon was slain by More of More Hall, which is to be found at the eastern end of More Hall Reservoir at Wharncliffe. The dragon's den was at Wharncliffe Crags.

There is a North Country legend of Gabriel Ratchet's Hounds – a pack of demon dogs which pursue the souls of the damned across the sky. The story was probably inspired by the eerie sounds made by night-flying migratory geese. Some tales of monsters may have been made up by parents anxious to prevent their children from straying into lonely places, others were folk-memories of wolves and other wild beasts which once roamed Britain. Others are not so easily explained. Of all the pagan deities, the woodland spirit was the longest-lived. Variously called *The Green Man* or *Jack-in-the-Green*, he is commemorated in pub signs and depicted in medieval churches as a demonic composite of man and tree. He may still live in Sheffield.

There were also fiends called bar-guests, boggarts or boggards. Usually an omen of death, they came in various forms – a white cow or horse or an enormous black or white dog with huge paws, shaggy hair and glaring, saucer-like eyes. Sometimes they came in human form, when they were particularly malicious, though there are tales of boggarts helping farmers to thresh the corn.

have drowned herself in the boating lake, when her father refused permission for her to marry the man she loved. Archie Roy, Professor of Physics and Astronomy at Glasgow University, said in 1987 that it is a common myth that ghosts are transparent shadows. They often look like ordinary people. They wear ordinary clothes, even cast shadows and are visible for several minutes. They are not necessarily surrounded by a cold atmosphere. Some even carry on conversations with passers-by. It is only when they suddenly disappear or are recognised as a dead person that people realise the truth. If they were pleasant people in life, it is unlikely they will do us any harm.

One theory is that ghosts are figments of the imagination. Often under stress a mechanism is triggered off in our minds to produce full-blown three-dimensional hallucinations.

Graves Park

....

JUST OVER THE wall from Bunting Nook is Sheffield's largest park, through which used to run the stage-coaches to London. One of the coach and horses is said to still bowl along the old road.

The ghostly stage-coach has not been seen since the early 1900s, when a group of people saw it pass through the wall of the Lodge and the stone wall beyond to disappear into the mist across the park..

Many years ago an old lady was walking in the same section of the park between the Derbyshire Lane gates and Bunting Nook when she heard a child crying. Although she searched the area, she found no-one.

At the beginning of 1982 a man was

playing with his dog there. He threw a stick for the dog to fetch, but it whimpered and refused to fetch it. Then the man heard a whistling and saw what he had at first taken to be a tree, until he realised that it was in fact the greenish form of a man. It was much more distinct than the shape seen by the police officers in Bunting Nook. It continued to whistle, but there was no other dog in sight apart from the watcher's dog who was absolutely terrified. The watcher at last turned to walk away – and the Thing walked after him. He turned back and approached it, whereupon it backed away and disappeared.

Hell-Clough
Norton
....

TODAY ANYONE SEEKING the old tithe barn at Hell-Clough, off Lightwood Lane, Norton will have difficulty finding even the foundations just inside the wood. Certainly as he looks down across the field in front of it, he can have no notion that the peaceful scene was once the setting for a tragedy.

Harold Armitage wrote the story of the laird of Hill-Clough or Hell-Clough in *Chantrey Land*, first published in 1910, but he had taken it from an obscure poem published in a collection in 1903 by the then Vicar of Norton.

In 1745, James Archibald Durant was a Scottish laird living in the Hebrides. He was a kinsman of Cameron of Lochiel and a distant cousin of the royal house of Stuart. A man of hasty temper, he became jealous of his wife's kinsman. The lad lived with them and she treated him as a favourite pet, but her husband mistakenly suspected that they were lovers and stabbed the boy with his dagger. When the wife realised why her husband had slain him, she shrieked and dropped down dead on the same spot as her kinsman.

The islanders, outraged, threw out their laird, without waiting for a formal trial. It was at this time when Charles Edward Stuart landed in Scotland from France and called upon all true Scotsmen to join his army to fight the English. Durant seized the opportunity of honourable exile and signed over his estates to the kinsman, to whom they would fall by Scottish law of forfeiture if the owner were found guilty of murder. Taking whatever money and jewels he had, his claymore and his little daughter, Selina (or Madge, according to the Vicar of Norton), he joined the Prince in the invasion of England.

When the Scots retreated from Derby, with the English country folk picking off stragglers, Durant was forced to exchange his kilt for the uniform of an English grenadier (we can only guess at how he obtained the uniform). Wandering from the main line of retreat, in December he arrived at the *Hare and Hounds* at Hemsworth and asked the landlord, Joel Howarth, for shelter for himself and his child.

Despite his suspicions of the stranger, Howarth took pity on the child and let them stay for several months, until Durant bought some land at Hell-Clough from a farmer, a member of the Lindley family and with his own hands built a house of rough-hewn stones and obtained a license to sell 'beer, white ale, aqua vitae and Virginny tobacco.'

The house became a wayside inn
Though rude it was, and rough;
And, far and wide, all travellers knew
The 'Change House of Hill-Clough.'

The years passed and Selina grew into a beautiful young woman. The local swains came a-courting, but in the proud laird's eyes none were fit to wed his nobly-born Catholic daughter. However, Selina took to meeting in secret handsome Paul Latton,

the son of a Calvinist minister.

When the laird discovered the truth he was overcome with wrath and upbraided his daughter until she fainted with fright. As she was recovering consciousness, the unsuspecting Paul entered the inn, to be knocked down by the furious father.

Madge threw herself between them.

'Stay! Father, stay!' the maiden cried.
'Strike not my lover true;
For I have lov'd him long, and now
He is my husband, too.'

This infuriated the father even more, for not only was Paul unworthy to marry a laird's daughter, he had married her without her father's consent.

The Scotsman ordered Paul to stand up, saying: 'As lover thou hast ta'en a blow; as husband take thou this.'

He drew his dirk and Paul was forced to draw his own in self-defence. After a terrible fight the old man fell, pierced to the heart.

The maiden, stricken with the sight
Fell at her father's side,
And, in an agony of grief,
Throbbed out her life, and died.

The unfortunate Paul was forced to flee abroad to escape the law. The Change House of Hell-Clough eventually fell into ruins. But, although Harold Armitage and the good Reverend did not realise it, Madge still walks the field in front of her old home.

In recent years there have been several sightings. A certain school teacher was inclined to scoff even when he himself saw a white, female figure apparently rising out of a small pond at the top edge of the field. As he approached, the figure shimmered and disappeared. A mere mirage, he said, a trick of the eye.

A Norton Lees family were not so sure. Father, mother and nine-year-old daughter were walking one fine summer's day in June 1965 down Lightwood Lane. They passed some old Victorian houses. One of them had new window frames and a garden riotous with roses. The mother thought how the owner must love roses and imagined a woman in a long crinoline gown and a picture hat. In view of what they saw soon afterwards she wondered if the force of her imagination had somehow given substance to the ghost. Until the writer of this book talked to farmers in the area about what they had seen, the family had never heard the story of Madge nor that she had been seen by other people.

They strolled on up Packman's Lane and paused to look across a field high with corn. Across the field coming towards them they clearly saw a female figure. She wore a long, light-coloured gown covered in a flowery pattern and a big flowered hat which shaded her face. She was too far away for them to see her features clearly but they received the impression that she was young. The most startling thing about her was the way she appeared to be floating over the top of the corn!

About forty feet from them she walked into a small group of trees in a hollow and vanished from their sight. They waited for her to reappear. Nothing happened. After several minutes the husband decided to go down to investigate. He walked all round the trees and was in sight of his wife and daughter the whole time. He reported that there was nowhere the woman could have gone to. There was no path and moreover the corn over which she had moved showed no signs of flattening. Yet a flock of birds had flown out of the copse as she had entered it, as if frightened. The family tried to rationalise what they had seen. Could it have been old Mrs Isherwood Bagshawe, the eccentric owner of 'The Oakes', the large house in the vicinity, whom they had once before seen walking in the area in her long dress and straw hat? No, it was definitely a younger woman. In a field well away from houses? Besides, the style of dress, as they agreed later, was eighteenth century. They later heard that Mrs

Bagshawe had in fact died a year previously.

The reactions of the family are interesting. All were convinced that they had seen something out of the ordinary. The daughter was frightened. The wife felt excited, privileged. The husband remained non-committal. He felt there had to be a rational explanation. All were definite that they did not want their name published for fear of ridicule by their neighbours, but the wife said that she was relieved to know that others had seen strange phenomena in the same field.

Endcliffe Park

O N THE 23RD FEBRUARY 1944 local newspapers reported that an American Flying Fortress bomber, the *Amigo Mio* of 305 Bombardment Group H, 8th USAF, from the base at Chelverston, near Wellingborough, had crashed in Endcliffe Park killing all the crew of ten in a fierce fire. A monument in the Park commemorates the unhappy event.

The plane had crashed near the step-

ping-stones on the Porter Brook. About midnight on the 31st July 1985 John Atkinson was returning home across the park, when someone shouted, 'Hey! You!' He looked round to see the shadowy figure of a man near the stepping-stones. Even as he watched, the figure turned away and vanished into thin air.

Endcliffe Grove Road

Endcliffe

....

THE FLATS WERE BUILT in the 1960s in a field and the couple had lived in their two-bedroomed flat for ten years without incident until 1993. They have no idea what started off the unnerving happenings.

The wife's mother visited her daughter one afternoon, leaving her shoes, coat and shopping in the hallway. When she came to leave, she saw that her shoes had been moved and her coat and bag had vanished. They searched the flat and eventually found them dumped under the window in the spare bedroom – a room no-one had entered during her visit. The daughter then admitted that other strange incidents had taken place.

The most terrifying was when she was standing at the sink and saw the reflection of a woman in the window, as if standing behind her. Yet no-one was there. The reflection showed clearly a middle-aged woman with dark hair, wearing a red jumper. She looked very angry.

Since then the wife has awoken at night to the smell of cooking and the most beautiful perfume. She has also heard someone playing lightly on a drum and an eerie whistling.

A light bulb mysteriously unscrewed itself from the ceiling and crashed into pieces, a coffee cup suddenly upturned, spilling coffee onto the floor.

The ghost is also blamed for turning off the central heating and flicking switches.

A psychic friend was called in and sensed the presence of a woman. She gave them some holy water from Lourdes to sprinkle around the flat – to no avail.

The wife now avoids being in the flat alone at night. However, they have no intention of being driven out by the ghost.

Millhouses

Knaresborough Road

....

A TUNNEL RUNS from Beauchief Abbey to the old corn mill at Millhouses. It continued 200 yards to a well in the centre of one of three large cellars in a house in Knaresborough Road, where Frank H. Brindley, the local historian used to live.

The well was covered by a square flag with an iron ring in the centre. There were iron climbing bars down the well, thirty feet to where there were openings in the sides, like six-foot-high stone doorways complete with carved lintels. From the well the tunnel continued to the cellar of an old hall in Millhouses Lane.

There is a story of a monk seen coming from the cellar in Knaresborough Road. One tenant went to her doctor and told him that her mind must be failing as she 'saw things'. A later tenant, who had not heard of the ghost, saw it pass through a solid door and vanish in the cellar. Hearing her screams, neighbours came running thinking there was a thief, and found the tunnels. They were bricked up, but the nervous tenant moved out.

The next owner had the well filled in with rubble.

Bents Green

....

BENTS GREEN has its fair share of ghosts, although one at least seems to have been the product of overactive imaginations. The *Sheffield Independant* of 31st October 1887 reported how on a foggy winter's morning at Parkhead a Mr Chapman and Jacob Bradwell bumped into each other, scaring each other silly. There is, however, a legend of a phantom black retriever on the road in the same neighbourhood.

If a crow flies in a north-westerly direction from Park Head House over Broad Elms School (the area was once known as Broad Oaks) he comes to Ringinglow Road and Bents Green Special School, the old Bents Green Lodge and the scene of a tragedy.

The Lodge was originally built by Lord John Murray of Banner Cross in 1786 as a farm cum public house, *The Rising Sun*. It was the main inn on the Buxton Road. The landlord had a strong objection to hearing bad language in his house. One day, Anak Osborne had had too much to drink, and when the landlord told him to leave, he swore at him. The landlord followed him outside and, in a rage, seized the whip from his hand and struck him over the head

with the butt. Osborne fell down and the landlord thought he had killed him. So, to cover up, the landlord dragged him across to Whiteley Woods in front of his horses, who pulled the cart over him. He then carried him home.

When an inquest was held at the inn, the landlord stayed in bed, saying he was ill. The verdict was accidental death, that Osborne had fallen out of his cart in a drunken stupor. However, the landlord could not live with his conscience. His health declined and he let the business go to rack and ruin. On his deathbed he sent his wife for Rev. George Smith, curate of Ecclesall.

As Rev. James Wilkinson, Vicar of Sheffield Parish Church and a JP, was that day taking a service at Ecclesall Church, both he and Rev. Smith drove to Bents Green in the Vicar's coach to hear the confession. The landlord said that he thought that Osborne had moved even as the cart ran over him. His wife, in grief and shock, survived her husband by only a few months, leaving their small daughter.

Ever since, late at night a coach was occasionally seen with lamps lit and two clergymen inside, coming out of the Lodge gates. The Rev. Smith's grandson, Blakelock Smith, riding home one night, encountered the coach and spurred his horse after it, but it rounded a corner and disappeared. The approach of the Lodge is now altered and the old gates now walled up. The coach no longer appears.

The house fell almost to ruin for some years after the landlord's death, then, a pub no longer, it was bought as a private residence in 1814 by Mr Joseph Bishop and restored.

Mr Albert Smith, the son of the clergman, owned it from 1829. Osborne was said to haunt the cellar (looking for beer?), but Mr Smith got rid of him by the simple method of building a good drain! In 1929 the house was bought by the

Education Committee and opened as a open-air school for delicate children. At first it was residential, but after a year it also took day pupils.

In 1965, an extension was built and the old school remodelled to provide accomodation for about 210 delicate boys and girls. Now, however, it is retitled Bents Green Special School and caters for children with problems.

On one occasion before the Second World War maids called the caretaker to investigate strange noises, but he neither heard nor saw anything.

Holmesfield

•••••••••••••••••••••••

OLMESFIELD HAS some strange inhabitants. At Moorwood Hall Farm a woman locked up her house to attend her daughter's funeral. When she returned she found the house empty, yet it had been completely cleaned and tidied and a fire burned in the grate. She was certain that she had the fairies to thank for this good deed.

Once upon a time a Holmesfield man decided to call up the Devil. Arming himself with a frying pan and a key, he went to Four Lane Ends, where many people gathered to watch.

He chanted: 'I raised the Devil and the Devil raised me.

I never shall forget when the Devil raised me.'

There was a clap of thunder and the Devil appeared. Only the man could see him and he said: 'Get thee behind me, Satan, for it is written that thou shall worship the Lord thy God and Him only shalt thou serve.' The Devil promptly vanished.

Coal Aston Common is not far behind in spookiness. Three spectres can be seen

there. The first is of three thin women standing in line, each holding an hour glass. The second is of a nine-foot giant carrying an oak tree over his shoulder. The third is of a normal-sized man carrying a scythe. The meaning of these is as follows: the three women mean that the beholder has but three hours to live; the giant has come to inform him whether he be young or old; and the man with the scythe has come to cut him down.

Dore

••••••••••

N A LETTER to *Morning Telegraph* of 11th September 1937, seventy-seven-year-old Mrs S. Elliott, then of Crookes, described incidents in her childhood at Dore. When she was fifteen she was engaged in service at Ullett Hall, Dronfield, by a Mrs Dobbs, who was then the occupant.

Late one dark night, she had to accompany her across the fields, and when they were near the stile two fields from the Hall, they were startled to see the form of a headless lady walking alongside the hedge. When they had recovered from the shock, Mrs Dobbs said, 'Well, we have heard the story of the ghost of the headless lady, now we have seen her'.

On another occasion when she was a child, she and her sister were performing their weekly errand of fetching flour and bacon from a farm. Along Shorts Lane, Blacka Moor, they were amazed to see the apparition of two women walking together arm-in-arm on the road some way in front of them. Before the children arrived at a stile they intended to use, the women had disappeared.

Fulwood Head Farm

....

O NE THURSDAY IN JULY 1912 it was churning day at Fulwood Head Farm and Sarah Helen Silcock from Yarncliffe Farm was expected to come as usual to take tea with her aunt and exchange news.

That afternoon her uncle, Joseph Silcock and one of his men, Billy Howe were on top of a haystack in the stack yard and so could see very clearly anyone coming along the Head from Ringinglow.

Suddenly, Billy Howe exclaimed, 'Sithee, mester, there's your niece, Sarah Helen, coming to see her aunt You could nearly set your watch by her!'

'Aye,' said Joseph, 'she's a good lass'.

But as the figure drew nearer, Joseph was stunned to realise that he was looking at a phantom.

'She wasn't flesh and blood, but a spirit. I could see straight through her,' he later described it.

Billy Howe had also seen it and clutched at Joseph, crying out in alarm. As Sarah Helen came into the lane leading past the stackyard, they realised that she was a normal figure again and her greeting proved it.

The following afternoon came the news of a dreadful tragedy at Yarncliffe Farm, where Fred Silcock and his wife lived with their son, George and daughters, Ethel and Sarah Helen.

In the morning it had been fine, so the men were out gathering in hay, but after the midday meal dark clouds heralded another storm, so Sarah Helen, who had been helping to wash the dishes and was about to sit down with her mother to a cup of tea, said that she had better go and help the men.

She picked up a spare fork and ran into the field. As she reached a loaded hay wagon, there was a great flash of lightning and an ear-splitting clap of thunder. One of the men was hurled to the ground and the others stunned but they managed to stop the terrified horse from bolting. When they recovered their wits, they saw the partly incinerated body of Sarah Helen lying in a scorched furrow.

During the rest of the time that the Silcocks lived at the farm, they never mowed that field again.

Forge Dam
Whiteley Woods, Fulwood
....

I N 1938 THE GRAVES TRUST, created by local philanthropist Alderman J.G. Graves, bought the Forge Dam together with Old May House Farm to present them to the city in order to complete public ownership of the whole of the Mayfield Valley as a Green Belt along Porter Brook.

Forge Dam House was to be rebuilt to preserve the rural aspect when the new park was created along with an ornamental garden and tea-room.

The tea-room now stands on the site of the forge. There were two water-wheels to drive its tilt-hammer and blowers for the furnaces.

It was worked in 1799 by Messrs Thompson and Company but under Messrs Maxfield the dam was turned over to fishing, boating and swimming. From 1939, Mr and Mrs Goddard and family occupied the house.

A letter in the *Gazette* of September 23rd 1993 told of a mysterious incident in the summer of 1992. A gentleman took his grandson to Forge Dam. As he approached the cottage next to the cafe, he saw a lady sitting outside the cottage on a wooden chair, knitting.

He thought this was odd as the cottage had always appeared unoccupied. He glanced away and when he looked back the lady had vanished together with her chair.

So he and his wife were very interested to see a photograph in the *Gazette*, taken in 1951, of Mr and Mrs Goddard sitting outside the cottage on wooden chairs, the lady apparently knitting!

appeared.

About 1962 they did, in fact, cause an accident. The road has a bad record for accidents.

In 1986, a man looking down towards the stream was amazed at seeing a little gnome dressed in green, who was fishing there. The man scrambled down for a closer look, but when he reached the stream, the gnome was gone.

Others over the years have claimed to see Roman soldiers marching along the road, more than once causing motorists to swerve to avoid their ghostly presence.

Manchester Road
Rivelin

A GENTLEMAN TOLD HOW in 1906 his father was walking along Manchester Road near the junction with Rivelin Valley Road, when he saw a man in working clothes standing looking over a wall into a field near Rails Bridge. He looked away for an instant. When he looked back, the man had vanished. His son has subsequently seen the same man five or six times over the years in various spots in the same area. On one occasion he actually saw him vanish. On the other occasions he looked away for an instant and when he looked back, the man had gone.

Rivelin Valley Road

RIVELIN VALLEY ROAD is reputed to be haunted by a couple who were killed in a car crash there. Motorists have been startled to see them wandering across the road, and have swerved or pulled up to avoid them, only to find that they have disappeared.

Hathersage Road

UP AND DOWN Britain new legends are told. Phantom stage-coaches are still seen, but alongside them phantom lorries drive down motorways. Among the new legends is that of the motorist who picks up a hitchhiker only to discover at his next stopping place that his passenger has disappeared. Sheffield has its own version of this, as described in the 1965 Christmas issue of a Matlock weekly.

A courting couple were riding a motorcycle combination on a winter's evening between *Fox House Inn* and Sheffield. They were flagged down by a girl hitchhiker wearing a leather jacket and crash helmet. As she seated herself behind the man, she gave them an address in Sheffield. The couple continued on their way with their passenger.

It was as they were approaching the outskirts of Sheffield that the man realised that the girl was missing. Thinking she had fallen off and worried that she could be lying injured in the road, they returned the whole way to Fox House. There was no trace of her. They could do nothing but report the matter to the police.

They then returned to Sheffield where they decided to go to the address in Tinsley given to them by the girl. The door was answered by a lady who on hearing their story became very distressed. She told them that the description matched that of her daughter who had been killed in a motorcycle accident and had been buried only a few days before.

Main Road, Hathersage

Sangam's Balti Restaurant,
···

T HE RESTAURANT is situated in the middle of Hathersage opposite the bus shelter.

The building of which it is part has a date stone above it, '1952' with the logo of the Sheffield and Ecclesall Co-operative Society. Before that it was an antique shop. Kim Hartley bought it in October 1991, when it was 'La Taverna Rusticana' and

completely re-modelled it as 'Hartley's Bistro'.

Local historian Barbara Buxton discovered that the site was part of the 'Old Enclosures', *ie* pre-1808, according to maps related to the enclosures by Act of Parliament, which destroyed the ancient open field system. The enclosures were not completed until 1830. Maps show only one building then on that side of the road – a cottage or a barn. Photographs in the Francis Frith Collection show the next door cottages and maybe a couple of other buildings. Otherwise there were fields as late as 1902 up to the junction.

On New Year's Eve 1991, Hartley's second chef, Joyce Butterworth spotted the White Lady gliding through the kitchen and into the dining area.

'I was shocked to see her,' said Joyce. 'She didn't walk, she glided. I only caught a glimpse, but she was wearing something white, like a smock. It's possible it could have been a young girl. I don't feel she means us any harm.'

There is a legend of a young girl drowning in a nearby stream.

The first chef blamed her for the repeated disappearances of his watch, which he took off while working. It would re-appear a day or two later on some out-of-the-way shelf.

The Lady was also blamed for happenings in both the Ladies and Gents toilets. She was actually seen in the latter establishment. Taps suddenly turned themselves on at full blast at all times of the day, when no-one was there. Some mornings they found chairs knocked over at the same spot where Joyce saw her enter the dining area.

Since Christmas 1995 it has been owned by Amin Ali as Sangam's Balti Restaurant and the ghosts have been quiet.

Ghost 'plane over Millhouses

....

IN *THE STAR* of the 7th June 1995, Mr. S.R. Hartley told how he and two workmates were in the old Abbeydale Station yard (now the Beaucheif Highways Depot), when they saw, coming towards them from the west and driving steeply, a silver Dakota transport plane. One of the men, Harry said 'Its going to crash in Millhouses Park'. However, they heard nothing. Although they made intensive enquiries, they could not find out what had happened to it and there was nothing in the newspapers or on the radio.

Poltergeists

....

POLTERGEISTS have been reported from private houses in all parts of the city. They are particularly active in houses where there are adolescents and may be associated with one member of the family, reserving their attacks for him or her. In other houses the poltergeists are indiscriminate in their attentions. Occasionally they are proved to be spirits called up after someone has been playing with a Ouija board and perhaps neglected to break the glass containing the spirit at the end of the game, so that the spirit was unable to return to its own world. Sometimes a medium was unable to control the spirits he or she raised, but usually amateurs dabbling in black magic were the cause of their appearance. All too often no cause is known. Poltergeists here are distinguished from ghosts in that they do not take human form and are generally mischievous or malicious.

In the early 1950s a family in Upper Albert Road, Heeley regarded their poltergeist with tolerant amusement. The several adolescent children gleefully told all their friends, who visited the house in the hope of witnessing a performance. Among other tricks it would unfasten all the bolts on the back door after it had been secured for the night. A Chinese student, who was lodging there, became so nervous that he fled the house, refusing to go back.

Gabriel Hounds

....

THERE ARE MANY LEGENDS of demons in the form of animals. These are not the often friendly ghosts of dead pets. Dogs especially were a warning of an imminent death. The cries of the Gabriel Hounds sent shivers down many a spine.

In 1861 Mr Holland wrote, 'I can never forget the impression made upon my own mind when once arrested by the cry of these Gabriel hounds as I passed the Parish Church of Sheffield one densely dark and very still night. The sound was exactly like the greeting of a dozen beagles on the foot of a race but not so loud, and highly suggestive of ideas of the supernatural'.

Warnings of Death

....

GABRIEL HOUNDS are not the only harbingers of death. A lady once wrote to *The Star* about her experience.

She had been out dancing with friends. Returning home, she got into bed beside her mother and lay awake thinking about the evening.

Bright moonlight shining through the window illuminated the ornaments on the dressing-table. Downstairs the clock chimed midnight. Then she heard it – an unearthly sound – someone or something was climbing the stairs, wearing shoes with flapping soles that cracked and echoed like whips!

Her eyes became riveted to the open doorway as she lay stiff with fear.

'Whoever you are,' she whispered, 'please go away!'

But the phantom footsteps only grew louder. Then, as she was close to tears, the sounds suddenly ceased. Her mother was sleeping soundly and she could hear her brother's breathing from the next room. They had heard nothing.

The following morning she told her mother what had happened. Her mother was apparently quite calm.

'They say it's a sign of death,' she said, 'but don't worry. Nothing will happen to hurt us.'

However, when she arrived home that evening, her mother told her, 'Your uncle died on his way to work today; you must have heard the warning.'

For a long time afterwards she lived in fear of hearing the warning again, but she never did.

And finally, what of our resident ghost?

....

I N *MORE SHEFFIELD GHOSTS* I wrote of the ghost in the attic of our house in Meersbrook. We can always tell when it is in residence. Our now deceased female cat, Purdy, liked to snooze away her days on a bed in the attic, but when the ghost was around, suddenly Purdy wouldn't even venture into the attic.

We had always thought of our ghost as a little old lady, judging by her footsteps. However, even as *More Sheffield Ghosts* first appeared in the bookshops, another ghost, no doubt having read it, and been highly amused by it, decided to set the record straight.

On October 1st 1987 my husband and I and our sons were watching television in the evening in the sitting room. Our two cats were sleeping on the occasional table in the middle of the room. Suddenly, Purdy woke up and started walking round and round on the table, all the time looking at something in the middle of the table. She then peered under the table. She leaped across to a settee and walked across the back of it onto the other settee, all the time staring at the middle of the table. Eventually she settled on the back of the second settee, but continued to watch the table for several minutes. Her brother, Bodie slept through all this, but we humans were so puzzled that we stopped watching the television to watch the cat. One son said, half-jokingly, 'She's seeing the ghost!'

On October 3rd I returned home and went straight upstairs to change my shoes. It was 9.40pm when I started to come down the stairs. The landing light was on but the hall below was in darkness as the rest of the family were in the sitting room. I had gone down only two steps, when suddenly coming up towards me was a woman about fifty years of age. She had very dark hair, a squarish face and strong but pleasant features. There was a twinkle in her dark eyes as she looked straight at me. She wore a short-sleeved black satin dress covered in a pattern of small flowers. She was of medium height and her right hand rested on the banister. Her head and the top part of her body were very clear but she faded away from the knees down. As I watched, she took two steps up towards me. Then I blinked – and she was gone.

The next day I told my neighbour on the other side about the ghost. He had lived there since 1939. As soon as I described her, he said 'Mrs Roper!' The Ropers had lived at our house from 1934 to 1940. She had died of cancer about two years after they moved away. She and his wife had been good friends. He described her as a nice lady. Indeed I too had the same impression of her. At the time I was too startled to be frightened and thinking back I knew only a desire to know her better. I felt privileged to have seen her. Why did she haunt our house? Probably she was in the early stages of cancer when she lived here.

We had not felt the presence of Mrs Roper or the old lady in our house for several years and Purdy slept peacefully in the attic until her death in March 1995.

On Thursday 20th July 2000 at 10.30a.m I was coming out of the bathroom, when I glimpsed something at waist level dodging round the corner to the head of the stairs. It was the wide sleeve of a woman's dress made of a grey woven wool.

I looked round the corner but no-one was there. Yet I had definitely sensed a presence. My son was in his bedroom and my husband was in the sitting room. So was it our other ghost, the old lady, who until then had not ventured from the attic

level?

In May 1994 *The Star* revealed a possible reason for Mrs Roper's restlesssness. Her husband, Albert died in 1950, leaving his money, £20,000 to his friend and neighbour at Norton, Miss Constance Hazelby, having disinherited his son, John after a row. Constance invested the money, vowing that it should be returned to his family on her death. She died in December 1993, aged 89, when the money had increased to £200,000, but the Ropers had left Sheffield long since and no-one could trace them.

Epilogue

·····················

E NGLAND IS SAID to have more ghosts per square mile than any other country in the world. Could it be that Sheffield, unlikely though it may seem, is the most haunted city in this haunted land? Be that as it may, we have seen in these pages how the record of Sheffield's ghosts is a record of her history.

But this book merely starts you off on your search for our city's ghosts. Happy ghost-hunting!